Letter to Your Self

Wojciech Salski

Copyright © 2024 Wojciech Salski

All rights reserved.

ISBN: 978-1-8384997-9-2

DEDICATION

I dedicate this book to my parents,
whose love and guidance continue
to uplift me throughout my life's journey.

Table of Contents

ACKNOWLEDGMENTS .... **VII**

FOREWORD .... **VIII**

PROLOGUE .... **XI**

    Story 1 2

CHAPTER 1. WHERE ARE YOU RIGHT NOW **5**

    Story 2 9

CHAPTER 2. HOW ARE YOU RIGHT NOW **12**

    Story 3 18

CHAPTER 3. WHO ARE YOU RIGHT NOW **21**

    Story 4 27

CHAPTER 4. WHAT DOES IT FEEL LIKE **30**

    Story 5 36

CHAPTER 5. WHAT CAN WE DO WITH IT ALL **39**

    Story 6 48

CHAPTER 6. LIVE AND LET LIVE **51**

    Story 7 56

CHAPTER 7. MAKE A WISH **60**

    Story 8 68

CHAPTER 8. LOVE YOUR STYLE **71**

    Story 9 79

CHAPTER 9. DON'T THINK, JUST GO. **82**

    Story 10 88

CHAPTER 10. TIME TO GET REAL **92**

STORY 11 98

CHAPTER 11. WHERE ATTENTION GOES 101

STORY 12 107

CHAPTER 12. KEEP YOUR PLANS TO YOURSELF 110

STORY 13 119

CHAPTER 13. LISTEN CLOSELY 122

STORY 14 128

CHAPTER 14. SPEAK YOUR TRUTH 131

STORY 15 136

CHAPTER 15. DECISION TIME 139

STORY 16 144

CHAPTER 16. IN PURSUIT OF WISDOM 147

STORY 17 155

CHAPTER 17. NO MATTER WHAT 157

STORY 18 166

CHAPTER 18. THE FIRST STEP PARADOX 168

STORY 19 175

CHAPTER 19. TAKE IT LIGHTLY 178

STORY 20 187

CHAPTER 20. WITHOUT MEANING 189

EPILOGUE I

ABOUT THE AUTOR IV

EPIGRAPH

'He who says he can,
and he who says he can't,
are both usually right.'
~ Confucius

Acknowledgments

Above all, I wish to acknowledge the support and love with which my family—Anna, Marcin, Hanna, Tomek and my Granny—has been keeping me up and afloat on the rough seas of life, especially in the past few years. Without their unwavering assurance that 'come hell or high water, all will be fine,' I would have budged and stumbled many times over.

Special thanks go out to my dear brother Tomek, whose wizard-like skills and aptitude for quick learning of all kinds allowed the cover of this book to become real. It was long within my mind, but without your help, it would have stayed there.

It's important to note Trenton McLellan, whose graphic design skills made the few accents on this book's cover possible.

Finally, I would like to thank those wonderful souls all across the globe, whose wisdom shared via mediums of literature, podcasts, and online lectures, allowed me to grow and consistently become a better person since I left my parents' house eight years ago. Figures such as Marcus Aurelius, David R. Hawkins, Jordan B. Peterson, and Julia Cameron, to name a few, have been there for me when no one else was able to accompany my efforts. It may be unusual to thank strangers, or those long gone from the face of this world, but it is essential, in my opinion, to do so.

Foreword

As I sit down to write this introduction to what you're about to experience, I wonder what use one can make of a book like this one. I trust there are many blessings and miracles to be found in this little thing, but I can only guess how many of them are here for you. As 'you are the master of your fate and the captain of your ship,' so you have all the power in choosing and employing the ideas hidden between the lines of this happening of mine. I can only cheer you on in this adventure of yours and wish you all the health, joy, love, and wonder that one could attain in one's life.

Let me tell you what this book is not. I am a firm believer that life is too short to read books that would steal our time without offering us what we seek. There are plenty of writings to choose from, so I want to help you in making a wise choice 'your thing.' This book is not a 'recipe for success,' and if you ever encounter one that claims itself to be, I urge you to have the courage to doubt. The world is filled with opinions and noteworthy advice coming to us from all directions, but there is no 'one size fits all'; and so, I do not want to claim mine is any different. This book is neither very easy to digest, as it may initially appear. There are ideas and concepts written into these verses that helped me immensely over the past years, and so I hope to convey them to you. But to grasp them, you will have to open your mind and read between the lines sometimes. Please be vigilant, and I hope you shall find what you seek. Finally, this book is not a 'one-night stand' kind of book. If you're into these things, you may want to leave it here and go off in search of your next 'great fix.' To apply the thoughts conveyed in 'Letter to Your Self,' you will have to dedicate your time, thought, and action. As it has helped me, so it can help you, but to allow others to help us, we really have to first want to help ourselves.

Now, if you've gotten this far, I have a feeling you're committed enough to see it through. Or maybe you're still wondering whether this scribbled voice has anything worthy to say. Well, I do not know the answer to that question, but there is one thing I shall promise you at this point. If you read the stories, ideas, and thoughts explored on these pages with enthusiasm, openness, and a feeling of curious wonder, you will inevitably raise your levels of health, joy, love, and wealth. It is for this reason I have written these words, and it is for this reason I've decided to share them with the world. Finally, let me briefly explain why someone like me would write something like this and why you should even care. As for the caring part, I shall leave it to you, as there isn't much one can do to make another care about anything. I trust that in your heart, you do care for much more than you consciously choose to, but let's leave the philosophy for another day, shall we?

Initially, the idea for this book was focused on children and educating them about the power of the mind and mindfulness. I had a wish of writing something a little lighter, a little more fun, and less inquisitive. Of course, as it often does, my creativity, alongside the Universe and my Muse, quickly entered a different destination code, and we have shifted the course of this boat one word at a time. Writing is something I do for pleasure but also as a means of self-care. I am my own therapist on the pages, where I can digest and put into context the many faces of existence, I get to experience each day. And that is what happened with this book. I needed these words of mindfulness, love, encouragement, and advice, and so they have manifested themselves in front of my eyes with every tap on the keyboard. I didn't mean to write a book about self-care. I didn't mean to create a therapy-like experience for myself. I didn't mean to note down the few simple actionable steps that can help anyone be, do, and have anything they want. I didn't mean to, but I did. And I guess that's what this book ultimately is. A letter filled with love, appreciation, support, and thoughtful ponder. A letter from one friend to another.

A letter to your Self.

Sincerely,
Wojciech Salski

Prologue

My Dearest Reader,

Hello!
How are you today?
How does it feel to read these words, hearing the voice inside your head?
Or perhaps someone is reading them to you?
Wouldn't that involve two voices participating—one of your friends and one inside your head?
How does that feel?
Can you feel the little tingle inside your forehead already?

First of all, I just wanted to say WELCOME.
I actually feel like screaming it with a grand, big smile, so please make sure to read it out loud appropriately. It is great to have you here, and I hope we will get to experience an amazing adventure together! May I ask how old you are? Let me guess... fifteen? No, forty-five?! The truth is, it does not matter.

As long as you are able to read these words or listen to them patiently, you are old enough for what is to come. What you're about to experience is all about being yourself and observing who you are. That is why it is a book for anyone, anytime, anywhere. No matter the age, race, gender, or one's favourite food choice. As long as you're breathing, you will have plenty of fun with me today. So, are you ready? Take a deep breath, grab a glass of water to keep you company, and let's go! Before each chapter, I have written a little story, a kind of gift to your imaginative Self from mine—a conversation starter. I thought it might be pleasant for both of us to get the chance to first 'connect the dots' unconsciously, then dive into these topics ourselves, and hopefully find what we were meant to find!

Okay, here goes the first one…

'Peace comes from within.
Do not seek it without.'
~ Budda

Story 1.

Sitting in front of the vast sea, the boy wiped his forehead, freeing the skin from the numerous droplets of sweat. It felt nice to do so. It felt pleasant. It must have been just after six in the morning, early enough for his workmates to still be asleep and calm. 'Calm,' he thought, 'that's what I need right now...'

It had been a while since he had seen his family and friends from back home. It had been a while since he had had the chance to speak with them face to face and laugh at the silly jokes made throughout the conversation. It had been a while since he had left home. Imagining what they had been up to, he relaxed his shoulders and softened his gaze. His forehead smoothed, his breathing slowed, and his twitching and moving subsided. He fell silent.

He closed his eyes and focused on the sound the waves made as they engaged with the coastal sand. Endless in and out. A patient and consistent rhythm of the world's breathing. He could hear the seagulls flapping their wings and gathering on the shore with the single aim of finding some scraps left by the last night's visitors. He could hear the wind's soft breeze as it swooshed across the coast there and back in a constant dance and swirl. He could hear the city of Kuwait slowly but surely waking up from the night's slumber, with the many traffic echoes, distant discussions in a language yet to be mastered, and tumultuous expressions of human civilization coming alive.

His mind quietened a little more, and so he focused on the sensations. He could feel the sand underneath his bare legs. He could sense the subtle sweat arriving onto his skin under the influence of the Middle Eastern warmth. He could feel the sun's early morning beams caressing his face and exposed parts of skin, making a world of difference to his rather sluggish state of awareness.

'Charging batteries,' his mind whispered, 'it's pleasant, isn't it...?'
As his meditation continued, the boy sat there cross-legged, slightly hunched over, quiet, and disciplined. It was a way of taking care of the body and the mind in a way that would allow him to tackle the challenges of the upcoming day in a manner much swifter and less distressing. It was the act of invigorating the spirit, allowing the space for thoughts and peace of mind in a world so troubled and way too hasty in its activities. It was the boy's way of 'putting on the armour.'

'To fight the dragons of today,' his mind smiled humorously, 'to be the best one can be, no matter the circumstances...'
He could hear the waves softly crashing onto the shore and feel the breeze carelessly moving his hair. He could feel his body loosen, his mind becoming quiet, and his breath becoming more and more peaceful. Minute by minute, he was becoming more 'here' and less 'out there.'

After a few more breaths, the boy slowly opened his eyes, gave the sea one last look for the morning, and got up. It was time to get back, make breakfast, write a few words, and get to work. It was time to get 'out there.' 'Never forget,' his mind echoed the long-remembered idea, *'wherever you are, be there..."*

Chapter 1. Where Are You Right Now

Okay, to start, we are going to need a moment of focus, so make sure to put your phone aside and turn that TV down to minimum. It's best if you take my advice seriously, as it will be easier to pay attention without these things bothering you. Where are you right now? Is it your bedroom? Are you in the living room, maybe? Are you on a plane or a train to somewhere? Are you sitting or lying down? Or maybe you're actually walking while reading?! Watch out for other people and do not cross the road without checking for cars, please! Wherever you are, I would like you to take a moment and observe this place. What can you see? Notice the colours, the shapes, the people, and things that surround you. Is there anything interesting? Did something catch your eye? Look around and name a few things you can see right now. You can write them down on the side of this page or simply say them out loud as you continue choosing. Who is there with you? Are you alone? Do you know the people around you, or are they complete strangers to you (maybe because you are sitting on a bus)? Tell me something about them. Is there anything you like about their looks? What do you think about this place? Is it nice? Would you like to be here longer, or would you rather go somewhere else? Is it a space you feel good about? Do you feel happy here?

Okay, enough with the looks. Let's notice the smell now. You can close your eyes for this part, but you don't have to. It's up to you! Either way, it will work well. Before you close them, however, make sure to read the questions I am about to ask you! What can you smell? Anything in particular? Do the smells you feel remind you of something you know from elsewhere? Do you like the smell of the place? How does it make you feel? What does it remind you of? Take a moment to really smell the place. Extra points if you can smell yourself at the same time!

Alright, are you happy with your smelling time? We have one more sense to explore before we get to feel how the world feels to us. It's about time we listen in. Yes, you guessed it! We will close our eyes for this one and keep them closed for as long as we wish. It is all about really listening in and hearing what needs to be heard. So, before you do close these beautiful eyes of yours, make sure to read the questions I have for you this time. First of all, I want you to simply hear anything and everything that can be heard. Try to name the different sounds your ears notice. Become a master of hearing. Hear it all! Can you hear someone's voice? Maybe your ears catch the sounds from the outside? Any particular rhythm you can spot around you? How about your heart – can you hear it beating? Do you hear your breath going in and out of your body as you calmly experience this space around you? Focus on these for a few moments and make sure to note them down in your mind. I want to hear all about what you heard today!

Finally, let's focus on what you can touch. You don't have to keep your eyes closed anymore, by the way. It would be surprising if you had them closed while reading these words, but who am I to decide on that! Okay, so what can your body feel? Are you sitting on something? Are you leaning on anything? Maybe you can feel people pushing you left and right as the bus meanders through the streets... Anyway, try to name at least five ways or things that you touch. Try to feel them if you can. Of course, do not touch anyone around you if they are not your friends! We don't want you to get in trouble. Write down what kind of touch you can notice.

Alright. It's time to think about what just happened. You have followed my invitation and focused on the way your eyes, nose, ears, and body feel the space you are in right now. In other words, you have become aware. Like in school, when the teacher asks if you are present, you were present in this space, by seeing, smelling, hearing, and feeling it exactly how it appears to you. You have really explored the moment you are living in. Quite cool, eh? Believe me, this is just the beginning…

Just remember to often take notice, where you are right now.

'Take care of your body,
it's the only place you have to live.'
~ Jim Rohn

Story 2.

The room was almost silent that evening. It must have been the weekend, as not many cars rumbled their engines outside the window. Citizens were already either in bed, getting to sleep, or watching some newly premiered blockbuster in the alcove of their homes. Tucked in, with the duvets on top of their socks-covered feet, the public had become the audience. Immersed as they were, it was likely they wouldn't notice anything about the world around them at all... This was not the case for the girl.

She too was tucked under a duvet in the cosiness of her living room, but the screen of the TV was off. Quite frankly, almost all sources of light were off, apart from the small incandescent lamp located just above the left corner of her sofa. She was wearing her reading glasses and sipping camomile tea from time to time, while her gaze draped the verses of the book's page. She was not much of a fast reader, but she had nowhere to hurry, and so she didn't see the point of straining herself to do so. She was simply reading. Leaning against a folded pillow behind her back, she balanced within the body's comfort zone. It wasn't easy to find the right sitting spot, as her back would often refuse to continue keeping the position for longer than a few minutes. It was nothing major, but overall, she found it a little distressing, especially when the pain would suddenly arise and stay there, squeezing the spaces around her spine for more than a few seconds. She was not old or troubled by any particular condition. It was just that with all the sitting her work and daily activities involved, she often found herself in pain at the end of her day. And so, she did that night. She turned the page and frowned, trying to ignore the discomfort beneath her lower back. 'Alright', she sighed, 'I'll move'. She shifted her weight once more and adjusted the pillow accordingly. The next few minutes' countdown began. There was no doubt that her backache troubles were becoming the norm. In this day and age, there was more and more sitting with less and less movement, which was taking its toll on the physical propensities of the human body worldwide. Those who were lucky or smart enough to take care of their bodies early in life and continue the practice were more prepared for the sedentary work, which was to fill their time after studies, but for the most part, people simply got on with it, often wincing with pain sporadically and trying all the remedies available to dismiss the uncomfortable pinches and pains. She continued reading for some time, before coming to a halt and once again changing the posture. She took a sip of the tea, looked outside the window, and focused her sight on the book once more. And then it dawned on her.

Something a friend told her once, when they were out and about, talking about monks from a faraway land and their unique abilities to be pain immune. 'Some of them would burn themselves on the street in protest against violence, and they wouldn't even scream', her colleague exclaimed back then, 'it's as if they were not feeling it at all...'. She pondered this idea for a moment. She thought of the discomfort in her back and of the things she could do to emulate the mentioned spiritual warriors of the world. She took a deep breath, closed her eyes, and focused her attention on that place where the pain felt the most vivid; most real. Her intention was simple – to alleviate or at least lessen the suffering. She continued breathing deeply, in and out, in and out, and feeling into the spaces that groaned and cracked with discomfort. Without having much *expectation to begin with, she was able to dismiss the major weight off the shoulders of her strained body slowly but surely. 'It is working', she noted silently, 'it hurts less now…'*

Chapter 2. How Are You Right Now

If you've found the last chapter a little difficult, do not worry. It is no surprise many of us do not know what to think of this when we encounter it for the first time. It's a part of our nature, but we have come to forget all about it over the past millennia. It sounds a little silly just to listen in, but that's exactly what we are here for, aren't we – to have fun and be a little silly! So, do not worry and carry on! You are doing great!

This time, I am going to ask you to tell me how you are feeling right now. There are no wrong answers here, so do not worry! We will try to find out what your body is experiencing and play a few games to see if your super-genius brain agrees with what your body tells it. Sounds good? Okay, follow me!

First of all, I want you to place your right hand on your chest, where you think the heart is. No, not that hand – the right one! Okay. Keep your hand there and try to feel your heart beating. Can you do it? Easy, right? Feeling this, let us close our eyes for a moment and observe this heartbeat symphony. How does it feel down there? Is your heart beating fast or slow? Can you count the times it bumps against your hand? How does that feel? Do you like this sensation? Have you noticed it before? Feeling into your heart can be a little tricky sometimes. That is why I am here to help you. As we continue on our journey, I will try to show you how you can always feel your heartbeat, even when your hands are busy doing something else. It is really fun when you get to learn it, because you can always remind yourself about this amazing heart of yours and its support. It is always beating; it is always there for you. Like your breath and your tummy, it is always making sure you are okay. The heart is a great friend of ours, so let's make sure we give it the love it deserves. Close your eyes and try to imagine how your heart looks inside, beating and keeping you healthy all your life. Imagine you hug it and kiss it on the cheek. It deserves your love. Make sure to let it know you care.

Alright, let's shift our attention to our breath. Similarly to the heart, your breathing is always there as well. It is so great to breathe, yet we seldom realize its awesomeness. We tend to forget and leave unnoticed the things we take for granted. Do you remember about your breath? Do you think about it often? Of course, I don't mean you should go crazy about it and constantly observe it… You have better things to do, I bet. Friends to meet, games to play… But it's important to note it is there and remember it from time to time. Alongside your heart, it is a companion that always participates in your adventures. They are always there for you. Your personal bodyguards. Guardian angels. So, can you feel it? What do you think of it? Do you feel yourself breathing deeply or rather shallow? Is it a quick breath or a slow one? Can you feel how your belly grows bigger each time you inhale? Can you notice the movement of your chest when you exhale? Let's observe this for a moment. How does it feel? What do you feel? Want to play a game?! How about we count the breaths in one minute…? You can ask your friend or a parent for help with measuring the time, as you count these cycles. Remember that each inhale and exhale count as one. They come in pairs, like shoes or gloves. So, take a moment and count how many breaths there are in your minute right now.

You got it? Okay, now write this number down and multiply it by 60 (yes, your parents can help you). Ready? Now, multiply it by 24. How much is it? A lot, right? Can you imagine this is about the number of breaths you take every day?! How crazy is that? This breath is a real worker, isn't it? A hard worker for sure. It's important to remember about this hero of breath we all carry around and turn to it whenever we feel overwhelmed with the world around us. Whatever happens 'out there', you can always take a few deep breaths and take a moment to feel your breath. It will help you get back to yourself, keep calm, and think more positively, even if you've had a bad moment or a sad experience. Like the heart, it is a great friend of ours that can always bring us closer to the moment and away from our worries. Remember about Mr. Breath and think of him often.

Okay, so we've noticed our breath and we've seen our heart's work. It's about time we feel into our brain a little. This task can be slightly confusing. Feeling into our brain might sound like a science fiction tale, but trust me, it's as real as the heartbeat you just felt. Let's try something a bit playful to tap into the workings of our minds. You're going to love this one!

Firstly, I want you to imagine that your thoughts are like little bubbles floating around inside your head. Some bubbles are big; some are small. Some are brightly coloured, and others are a bit dull. Now, without opening your eyes, I want you to reach out and 'pop' a thought bubble. Go on, give it a try. Did you pop one? Good! What thought was inside that bubble? Was it a to-do list item? A memory? A worry? Or perhaps something pleasant like looking forward to something exciting? It's fascinating to see what pops up, isn't it?

Now, let's take it a step further. I want you to visualize a conveyor belt moving through your mind, carrying all sorts of thoughts. Some thoughts may be worries about the future, while others could be fond memories from the past. Watch them go by without grabbing onto any of them. Just observe. This practice can help you realize that you are not your thoughts; you are the observer of your thoughts. By distancing yourself from them, you can gain a clearer, more mindful perspective.

Another fun activity involves playing the role of a mindful detective. Throughout your day, try to catch your brain in the act of thinking. When you notice you're lost in thought, silently say to yourself, "Gotcha!" and then gently bring your focus back to the present moment. This can be particularly amusing and enlightening, revealing just how often our minds wander away from the here and now.

Lastly, let's explore gratitude with our brains. Think of three things you are grateful for right at this moment. It could be as simple as the air you breathe, the comfortable place you're sitting, or a recent interaction that made you smile. Feel that gratitude deeply, letting it fill up those thought bubbles and noticing how it changes the quality of your mental landscape. Gratitude has the power to shift our focus from lack to abundance, from negative to positive.

Remember, the goal of these activities isn't to stop thinking altogether—that would be impossible. Instead, it's about becoming more aware of our thoughts, emotions, and bodily sensations. By mindfully observing the workings inside our minds, we can choose responses rather than reacting out of habit. It empowers us to live more fully in the present moment, enhancing our well-being and deepening our connection to life. Keep playing with these activities, and you'll discover the infinite possibilities within your own mind.

After all, it's all about figuring out how are you right now…

'Knowing yourself is the beginning
of all wisdom.'
~ Aristotle

Story 3.

No one kid is better than the other in anything, unless they start to practice it or are given the chance to learn the thing by mimicking their parents. Everyone has particular tendencies and hidden talents when they join the Earthly plane, but unless these are discovered, they remain just that – hidden talents without much worth. Unless they are unlocked... This was the case with the boy as well.

From a young age, he tried to do all kinds of things, most of which were interesting only up to a certain point and successful until the loss of enthusiasm. He would try dancing, playing football, singing, reciting old poetry, drawing with one of his eyes closed, or skating. In other words, he was trying it all. His parents were decisive about one thing from the very beginning – "one has to do something, have some passion or a hobby." "Otherwise," his mother would often say, "you won't find your spark." As much as the boy didn't understand it at the time, she was quite right. By being exposed to so many different activities and interests early on in life, he had the chance to experiment, learn, get enthusiastic about something, or find out it was simply "not for him." The activities were often an extra after the school time, which wasn't always the most pleasant thing for him, but as he grew older and had more and more opportunities to taste, consider, and discard these hobbies-to-be, he learned that finding what isn't for us is a necessary part of noticing what is ours to do, become, or have. With this attitude in mind, he slowly narrowed the field of focus in terms of his academic interest, after-school passion, and free-time fun. As the years of hanging around with friends and "joining the tribe" of rebellious youth rolled in, the boy was certain about at least one part of it all – stories. From watching to reading, from writing to telling, his interest in words-fuelled creativity was the one thing that brought him joy and pleasure, even in an academic setting. Other classes were, all in all, rather dull or too repetitive for him to care about. This, of course, brought around the challenging notion of "growing up" and "monetizing" this passion of his. "There is no money in books these days," someone would say. "You're better off studying medicine," claimed another. There were many voices against the idea of exploring the education connected to art, which was so utterly difficult to measure and so easy to disregard. These were difficult choices back then, but thanks to the boy's family and his stubbornness of purpose, he decided to follow the intuitive choice anyhow. And so, as it usually happens when one does not leave any other option but for the Universe to accommodate its magic to the needs of the determined individual, he got his way. True, there was rarely a time when his journey was an easy one. Moreover, on multiple occasions, his work, however good it may have been, was simply criticized, undermined, or dismissed. Nevertheless, with the idea fixed in his mind and the thought of a title he wanted to attain and emulate in mind, he was pressing on with unwavering certainty. He was determined to get where he was heading, and so he got his way in the end...

Time passed and reflecting on his early steps and the most difficult parts connected with beginning the journey, he noted one particular thing, which was most likely of greater importance than anything else in terms of his success. One could call it belief, another a delusion. Whatever it shall be called, it was available for the taking for every person worldwide. As it was once said, "to think what you want to think is to think the truth, no matter the circumstances..." And as he thought this truth of his and did what had to be done, he made it true in the end, and that has made all the difference...

Chapter 3. Who Are You Right Now

When it comes to understanding and appreciating ourselves, we are often the last ones to really try and make it work. Our parents love us unconditionally, but even this expression of love's greatness does not convince us of the truthfulness and worthiness of ourselves. We doubt if we can be loved. We doubt our strengths. We doubt ourselves. Whenever faced with difficulty or a challenging scenario, we fall into the hole of worry and comparison with others, who often feel just the same; if only it would be okay to talk about these feelings more... Realizing this universal tendency of humans to doubt, be concerned, and try to improve their ways is the first step to understanding and truly appreciating who we are and could become. We are problem solvers. We've always been. That is why we are more likely to find a problem worth solving than to stare at a solution when it is done and dusted. There is no potential growth in a solution-based gaze, so we turn our eyes to what is next to be done and carry on. One problem at a time. One challenge at a time. Although this is a quality that made our civilization so successful and allowed us, as a species, to conquer the planet and even some parts of the cosmos, we rarely notice the unfriendly quality that is carried with this proneness to problem-solving. We. Are. Always. Trying. To. Find. A. Problem. To. Solve. That's right, you heard me! We are always trying to find a problem to solve. Isn't that crazy?! What does that say about us? Do you think we are likely to find it if we look for it well enough? Of course, we are! That's how this game works! "Seek and you shall find," the scripture tells us.

Whatever you are looking for, one way or another, will be found. And since we are constantly looking for problems to solve, by nature, the majority of what we see is just that – problems. Even though there may be a myriad of wonderful successes, pleasant things, and loving surprises everywhere around us, because of our inner filter for problem-solving, we are likely to let them stay unnoticed as we try our best to find something worthy of our solution. Yes, I know what you think... It is quite a crazy thing. But here's the fun part. Since we know about it now, why don't we make a conscious effort to change this scenario!? Let's flip the script! Why don't we look 'on the bright side' and truly focus our attention on what is already solved, offered, and available in our lives right now? "As within, so without," the old books tell us, so let's start with ourselves.

Take a moment now and consider these few questions. You can write down some of your thoughts on the next page, as this will help you realize your amazing situation even better. What are you great at? What is your talent? Maybe you can do something no one else can! Did you show this talent to anyone, or is it a mystery? What comes easily and naturally to you?

For example, I find writing very pleasant and easy. I consider it to be my talent. What is yours? What do you like to do the most in the world? What could you do all day and not get bored or tired of? What makes you want to jump and dance and make all those crazy happy noises people make when they are so happy to be doing what they love? What makes your heart smile? What do you help others with? This may be the same thing you're great at or something completely different. Think for a moment. It's a difficult one. What do other people come to you for? What can you offer advice on? What are you an expert in? Write down anything that comes to your mind. Don't worry if some of these things feel small or unimportant. Just write them down and let it go.

Let's continue. What would you like to be better at? What would you like to improve? Focus on one thing for now! Only one thing! What would you like to master? What is it that if you were able to ask a genie in a bottle for, you would, and you would love the fact that now you can do it without any problem? Write down all the answers to the questions above and think about them for some time. You can take a break and grab another glass of water as you mull over these thoughts and ideas. Remember to stay hydrated as we continue on our journey! I don't want any dehydrated comrades in my crew!

List all your answers and take a moment to choose one or two that feel the most true and powerful to you. Can you decide which one of these is the closest to your deep aspirations and love for the world? For example, if, like me, you've written writing or telling stories in one or more questions and if you feel like that is what makes you the happiest, what comes easily to you or what you would like to become a master of, you can consider yourself to be 'a writer' or 'a storyteller'. I know you will probably say now "but wait, just because I want to do it, doesn't make me a writer just yet", and I understand your point. But remember, we are only getting started and the first step to realising our dreams and making ourselves happy is to believe that it is possible to do so. That is why, whatever amount of writing you have done up to this day, I want you to call yourself a writer from now on. If it feels like you, it is you, you just need to show yourself and the world the truth. We will get to that, don't worry. For now, choose which of these things describe you best and write it at the bottom of this page. "I am happy and grateful to be such a great…" Fill it in! You won't regret it!

After all, you may find it useful to realise who you are right now…

[WRITING PAGE]

'Make time to follow your passion,
and never let your hobbies and interests take a back seat.'
~ Richa Dwivendi

Story 4.

"Did you hear that by simply listing your goals and dreams, you greatly raise the chances of making them happen?" The question boggled the boy, as he realized he had not made many plans about anything in his life so far. He was already past his high-school and university years and working in a company that felt like the right fit for him, he did not hesitate much when asked whether he would stay in the job for longer. "Of course, I like it there," he would answer promptly. His friend waited for the boy's reaction, trying to decipher the shifting expressions passing through his face. There was no animosity connected with the idea, just some well-deserved care, as they both wished each other a level of self-fulfilment and success to play a part in their lively journeys. "I don't mean you have to sit down right now and write it all up, you know," he added after a moment of hesitation, "it's just that I thought you might be interested in this idea, as I am..."

They were sitting on the concrete wall outside the house of one of them. It was summer, and the weather was pleasantly warm, which meant the outdoor activities were in full force and the indoor experiences subsided substantially. The two were spending time together less often these days. One decided to move away and lived in a different country, whereas the other was already renting a flat with his girlfriend in the town they were both brought up in. One seemed to have it all sorted: a flat, a well-paying job, love to keep him company, stable pay, order. The other appeared to collect only stamps: a job here, a romance there, a flat to rent for a few months, a spontaneous journey elsewhere, chaos. "So..." the boy finally responded, "what kind of a list did you come up with over these past years...?" "You know, since you live with so much change all the time..." he added promptly. "Yeah, it's a good question, isn't it?" the other tapped his fingers against the wall, "I've had many lists since high school, and those are also constantly changing, you know..." "But for the most part, I have a few pieces for every aspect of life on them – from having to being, that kind of stuff..." The two mulled over the subject for some time.

"You know," the list-loving one started, "I also found it quite fun to do, writing the lists down and making plans, I mean." The other nodded without a word. "I guess not everyone likes to do it, though," he added, remembering the way his previous girlfriend used to panic whenever the idea of planning and dreaming of the future would arrive in their conversation. Sitting there, on that concrete wall, the two were far away from that space and time. One was recollecting the interactions with his love, whereas the other wondered about the plans he would make if such activity were to take place. Both of their foreheads slightly crunched; they looked like two sour-looking birds perched on one of the wire lines. "I think you should try it, you know," his friend added after some time, "writing the list, I mean, dreaming..." Later that day, the boy was at his flat, sipping a cold one and flipping from one movie to another on his VOD. He felt somewhat uneasy following the conversation. It did not feel as if they ever finished that chat. Not for him. With a slight hesitation, he pushed himself up and walked towards the bedroom, feeling the weight of anticipation dragging behind his steps. Drawing a pencil and a piece of paper from one of the drawers, he sat by the bed and, without much thinking, scribbled one word at the top of the page, 'GOALS'. With the enthusiasm of a sloth, he promised himself to write down at least a *few, maybe five, goals of somewhat important relationship to his life's joy. Upon beginning, he felt little stiff. It took him some time, but after the first few items, he warmed up and got to write it all out. He must have been doing it for at least an hour after all. The finished list was divisible into seven categories and three timeframes. He was that kind of person after all. He loved organizing, and once the activity kicked in, he was flying...*

Chapter 4. What Does It Feel Like

Thinking of these things can really boggle one's mind. It is often with this kind of thoughts that we forget to make ourselves feel okay with whatever comes up. It is about time we take care of ourselves in a loving way. Like the child you once were or still are, you need to take care of yourself for real! Try it for a moment. Write down a list of things that make you feel happy when you do them. They can be whatever you like to do, both what you're doing on a regular basis and what you've not done for a long time but feel like it was fun when you did it. Whatever these are, write them down below. As many as you can remember. As many as possible!
[WRITE HERE]

Sometimes the simple action of writing down or even thinking about certain things helps our heart to jump. However old you may be, there is still within you the same child you once were with the same kind of passions, dreams, and joys. All of us like to do something. All of us are passionate about certain things. All of us adore some silly pieces of life that others may find completely boring or absurd to think about. Do not worry about 'others'; focus on yourself. What do you like to do? What does it feel like to do it? When was the last time you had a chance to participate in that activity?

[WRITE HERE]

To focus on ourselves, we often need to get out of our 'safe space'. It may be difficult to see the whole forest when you're standing between the trees. We need to gain perspective. For this part of our adventure, you will need to remind yourself how it feels to do the things you like doing and put yourself in the shoes of yours from the last time you've had a chance to do them. For example, if you really love skiing, try to remember when the last time was you skied, what was so special about this activity, and what kind of emotions, sensations, and thoughts you had as you were going down that clean, white slope. For the description of sensations and emotions, feel free to come back to the first chapter as a reminder. Anyway, whatever you may write down or think about here, it will be fine. Just do your best to recall as many details as possible of 'what does it feel like' to do your favourite activity. You can write out and remember a few different ones if you're feeling extra motivated. This is a good task to do first thing in the morning because your mind is still clear and ready to quickly remember the past as you think about it. Do not watch any movies or news programs before you do this!

Okay, so you've listed a few activities and remembered one or two of them more specifically. Now, it is time to feel into this amazing thing you like to do once more. Close your eyes and imagine yourself doing what you love to do. Try to feel into the feelings your body is experiencing as you reflect on this activity. You are tricking your brain to think you are doing it, even though you may not be doing it for real. That's okay. It's all part of the fun. Put your imagination to work and really do your best in becoming the person you see in the picture of your mind. Do what you want to do and imagine it happening for real. Be excited about it. It may seem like a silly activity to do, but it is a good practice and a great way of improving your mood. For now, just focus on your favourite activity, take a few minutes, and fly!

[TAKE A MOMENT TO EXPERIENCE IT NOW]

How was that for you? Fun or boring? Some people find it more difficult to imagine things visually because they primarily think in words or sounds, others find this exercise highly stimulating, as it is in their nature to see pictures in their mind. Whatever your experience may have been, it is great you gave it a shot! I hope that this little exercise opens a new space for you to consider your activities and choices in the days to come. Anyway, let's continue, shall we?

So, we've done some fun daydreaming and looked at the activities that make you feel happy, relaxed, or simply having fun. Remember these things because they are a part of you! They are what makes you unique. Some of us like spaghetti, others love chocolate cake, and me, for example, I like sushi a lot. It is all a matter of taste. Of course, you do not eat your snowboard or a teddy bear, but the personal preference that comes with choosing one or the other can be considered a taste for sure. We need to appreciate ourselves more because that is what gives us the power to show up true in this world. Each of us has something beautiful to offer to the world and recognizing that can really strengthen our abilities to be our best selves. I would like you to take a moment and think of the few things you feel you're good at. What can you do easily? Is either of these things on your previous 'I like to do' list?

Finding this can really help you choose the right direction for your life. What we are naturally good at tends to be a good starting point for choosing what we want to get better at. For example, if you're great at telling stories or presenting in front of the class, you may want to practice public speaking or writing more, and go in the direction of being a teacher, a writer, or a stand-up comedian. If, on the other hand, your strength lies in math and you just love turning those numbers in your head and coming up with solutions, exploring economics, physics, or chemistry may be the best way of taking advantage of your talents and passion. I know it can be difficult and a little overwhelming to make choices, especially when you are young and inexperienced. I must reassure you, however, that we've all been there and, quite frankly, there is no bad choice to make. As long as you try and go in a certain direction, instead of 'sitting on the fence', you will learn and see whether that direction was the right one. Sometimes, we have to learn what we do not like to find what we do enjoy. It's a journey; do not ever forget that!

Okay, in this short chapter, we've looked at the importance of finding what feels right for us. We are yet to explore the deep benefits of this kind of activity, but for now, it is important to note that when doing what we love, we are more likely to do it well. If you are passionate about something, you feel more inclined to learn about it, explore it further, and do more of it daily. And that is exactly what success and fulfilment look like. Finding your spark and building a fire with it is a great way of spending your days. Whatever fills your heart with joy, you should put in first place. Do not abandon other activities and do not leave school before your time to leave comes, but whenever you have free time, do something related to your passion. It will be both fun and truly wonderful. It can also be life changing, I promise.

Ask yourself, 'what does it feel like…?'

'With self-discipline
most anything is possible.'
~ Theodore Roosevelt

Story 5.

"Everyone knows the story of the turtle and the hare, in which the hare is beaten by the turtle in a race. One of them continues without a stop for many days, while the other makes all kinds of comments and prematurely enjoys the 'inevitable' victory over his opponent. In the end, the turtle turns up at the finish line before the hare, whose boasting and celebrating led to a great party just the night before. At least that's how I remember it," he explained, waving his arms in front of his brother's face. "Do you get the point?" a question followed suit.

Standing in front of the mountain, which they were to ascend in a few moments, the two were visibly tired. They had been walking for at least three hours, and there was, without a doubt, many more miles to go. They did decide to do so that day, however, so there is no need for you to feel bad about them. The sun was glancing at their faces with surprised appreciation, seeing the effort the two were giving in exchange for the views they were to experience. "I do, I get the point, but I don't see how this applies to me putting that hundred aside each month," the younger one finally responded. "Am I the turtle or the hare in this piece...?" "Or is that hundred the turtle maybe?" he added with obvious irritation. The older brother adjusted the position of the backpack on his shoulders and smiled with a grin of brotherly contempt. "Of course, the money isn't the turtle, you tool..."

As they got back to their walk, puffing and huffing deeply through the nose, as the exhaustion was slowly getting to them, the older one looked at the peak. "Do you think it's easier to get there in a short sprint or with a consistent, maybe slightly slow in one's view, effort...?" His brother looked up, squinted his eyes feeling the sun's lovely embrace, and shrugged his shoulders. "I guess it's easier to walk there slowly than to sprint, but who knows, man, there are all kinds of crazies in the world..." The two laughed. "Fair," the answer followed. "What I mean," the older started again, trying to make sure not to sound too patronizing with his explanation, "what I mean is that by making one step at a time, putting one hundred on the side each month, or learning one word a day, you can really make great progress over time..." "And time is what you have, bro," he added. "Time is all you have..." "Think of that hare and turtle story again," he continued. "The hare was obviously better equipped to win the race, but his attitude was wrong. He was so sure of the win he forgot to do what's necessary..." "And that's what I ask you to consider and avoid," he looked at his brother. "I don't want you to be so certain of all the time you have as a young man and all the potential that's still in you, that you do not take action already to make yourself better off in the future..."

The younger one stayed silent for a while. Their walk continued as they crossed one of the bridges and climbed a little hill towards the next great-view spot. There were still many steps to take, but they were visibly getting closer to their destination. Finally, a question echoed through the minds of the two. "Do you think he ever stood a chance of winning that race?" the younger one asked. "I bet he had," his companion smiled. "I think he was an obvious winner from the beginning, but with that kind of attitude, he was destined to lose..." "Do not let your pride, immediate gratification, or ego ever get in the way of your effort," he added. "Because if there is one thing that we can choose, it is our attitude, and without the *right kind of attitude, without a proper muscle of persistent effort, without controlling ourselves, we are like that hare... Proud too early and successful too late."*

Chapter 5. What Can We Do With It All

Realizing what we like to do and finding ways of being more aware of our bodies, minds, and thoughts is great, but it doesn't always seem to make much sense in the bigger picture. "Why should I observe my thoughts?" someone may ask. "What does it have to do with being happier?" another question might follow. There are many ways in which these activities will help us understand and be better with ourselves, but before we decide whether it is worth it, it would be useful to make sense of what we hope to gain from it all. What can we do with it?

Well, when it comes to being more mindful, there are two major advantages already documented by research, centuries of practice, and the oldest traditions of the world. Firstly, by becoming more aware of who you are and what is happening with you in the present moment, you experience less anxiety, which is a big thing, considering the current tendency towards more and more stress all around us. We live in a fast-paced, very intense, and often worrisome world, which causes us to feel preoccupied, anxious, and stressed all too often. By becoming an expert on yourself, you will be better prepared to 'not react' when some situation spins out of control potentially causing you to feel reactive in a negative way. You will feel calmer under pressure, will be able to focus on one thing at a time with more professionalism, and simply be healthier, as stress will not be influencing your body and mind in the way it used to. Developing a strong mindfulness practice is a great knight's armour, each of us can wear. Like working out in the gym, with each training and successful push-up we do in our mind, we become stronger and better equipped to face the day's turmoil.

The second great advantage of becoming your own best friend is better choice-making. If you think about it, life is all about choosing. We choose all the time, every day, and in every possible way. When to get up; what to eat; who to see; what to do; where to go; how to comb our hair; which pair of shoes to wear, and so on. It is a constant choice festival. From the moment you wake up until going to bed at night, your day is filled with little, medium-sized, and big decisions, which participate in creating your reality. Maybe you have not thought about it before, but that's how it is. If you want to see it for yourself, take a moment now and write below the fifteen things you've already decided on today.
[WRITE HERE]

I bet you a pack of crisps that you had already made quite a few choices, one of which was to continue reading this little book. See?! Gotcha!

So, these decisions, which some may call a free will decision, and some may dismiss as luck of the draw, are truly creating our everyday life. We make them all the time, often not thinking much of it, since many of them have already become our habits. Realize that by becoming more self-aware, you will improve your decision-making. You will know what is best for you and choose accordingly. You may leave that fast food dish aside and choose a salad next time because you know now that what you are and what you want to be is a healthy person. All great change starts small, so feel free to use this in any way you wish...

Okay, so now you know the two major advantages to this self-knowledge thing... If you've not stopped reading by now, there is a chance you're enjoying this process. Well, that makes the two of us. On an adventure like this one, it is often fun to bring a friend along. Of course, it may be challenging for you to read together from one book, and I am far from inviting you to buy two copies straight away. Instead, in the upcoming exercises, you can try inviting someone from your family or a friend to do these exercises with you. They are going to be quite fun and great to share. Fun, like love, only multiplies when it is shared. So yeah, if you feel like it, grab someone to join you now, bring them a piece of paper and a pen, and turn the page when you're ready!

As we've explored earlier, becoming more aware of ourselves and our likes and dislikes can really help us be smarter about the choices we make each day. From the type of food, we decide to eat for breakfast to the university degree we decide to study, these choices have nothing to do with being objectively good or bad, and everything to do with our subjective point of view and the outcome we wish for from them. For example, you may want to eat a fast-food meal on a Saturday as a treat, and even though it is not the healthiest option, you can easily enjoy it. The trick is, however, to recognize this treat for what it is – a 'cheat meal,' and not try to convince ourselves that it is healthy and good for our body to make such choices every day. It is okay occasionally, but we should see it for what it is. If you're doing this to make yourself happy and treat your inner child well, that's great! Just remember what fast food is and do not try to convince yourself that having it for breakfast each day is a good idea. It just isn't!

The greatest part about becoming more self-aware is the fact that you will be better at recognizing these 'good' and 'bad' ways and you will be more likely to choose wisely when the time comes. Strong will is like a muscle. It gets stronger each time you use it, especially when it gets challenging. To practice this kind of decision-making, ask yourself what your mind and body feel about the food or choice you are about to take before you do. Each of us has a wonderful, almost magical compass inside, which often knows what's best for us, even before we decide to ask. Some people call it conscience, some call it a gut feeling, others – intuition. The way I see it, it doesn't matter how you call it; it matters how you use it. With good use of your inner guidance, you will likely avoid the things you should avoid and pay more attention to those you should focus on. It is a great tool, which you can take advantage of every day.

Okay, so as for the exercise I promised. Is your friend there with you? Grab a piece of paper (or you can use the space below) and write down all the activities you do in a day. Yes, you heard me! All of them! From the moment you wake up to the moment you fall back to sleep. What do you do in a day? You can take a weekday for this exercise because there are more of these in your life than weekend ones. Write down what activities and things you take part in throughout your day. What do you eat, where do you go, who do you see, etc. All of it. The more the merrier. I will give you a minute or two to do this before we take the next step.

[WRITE HERE]

[WRITE HERE]

Alright, you ready? Anything else that comes to mind? No? Okay, let's continue.

With these written down, take a moment now and reflect on each of them. Which of these activities are DEFINITELY good for you? Which of them would you advise your best friend to do? Which of them inspire you, make you feel happy, improve your life quality, make you feel your best, healthy, and fun? Give yourself a minute and mark them. Mark every activity that you can feel (yes, I say feel) in your mind and body to be a good one. Trust your intuition. Trust your inner compass. Mark all of these and then come back to me.

Now, as you have the good, fun, healthy, interesting, and inspiring marked, you may have a few left. Whatever they may be, ask yourself this – what do I get from doing them? What is the reward? How do they make you feel? Taking a moment to reflect on this, consider why you would want to continue with these and do not be shy to admit that you simply like how they taste, make you feel, or allow you to relax.

[TAKE A MOMENT TO REFLECT ON IT NOW]

There are no bad or good answers here. Be honest with yourself. Be honest with your friend. Allow both of you a space in which you can find the things that really are worth something to you and leave the ones that do not serve either of you. Of course, do not dismiss activities you are unsure about for now. Maybe, for the time being, you should continue with that cold shower, even though you are not certain whether it is a good or a bad thing for you, sometimes choice needs some time to mature, so please, do not rush it! Doing this exercise with a friend can be more challenging than on your own, but it will also be much more powerful and helpful in the long run. At times, we simply need someone else to notice what we have been turning our gaze away from. So, do not worry and carry on. Answer these questions and look at your list after it's all finished.

How do you feel about these things? How did you find the exercise? Was it hard, or maybe easy? Did you feel your intuition working its magic when you invited it to and listened closely to its answers? It often only takes a moment of silence and concentration to hear what our inner guide has to say.

Our world is very loud these days with advertisements, noises, opinions, and offers flooding our reality at every moment. It is difficult to be quiet and listen to ourselves in this kind of space. But it is possible. It only takes practice. The outcome of this exercise is two-sided. On one hand, you now know which things in the day you really care for and which you could probably let go of. On the other, you have had a chance to see how 'listening into yourself for help' works, and you can now use it in other parts of your daily life as you please. Remember, it may take some time before your

intuition muscle becomes strong enough to let you know its wisdom in real-time, and there may be moments when the decision at hand is too difficult for your intuition to decide on it promptly, but do not doubt that it is there for you, because it is. Always. Like a quiet teacher, a master of life, sitting behind your ear, your intuition is there ready to help you choose what is best for you…
It is always there for us to remind us what can we do with it all.

'Father, forgive them,

for they do not know what they do.'

~ Luke 23:24

Story 6.

"He takes ages to get ready in the morning, keeps smiling like a douche when we go into the meetings, and seems to care only about his free time whenever our workday is close to finishing," she listed with exasperation over the phone to her friend. Her co-worker went out for a run, which gave her the chance to talk openly with her loved ones without him being able to hear. "I don't get it," she continued, feeling the irritation climb step by step to the top of the annoyance tower, "why would you even take this job if you know you're going to be writing a book, making a podcast, and training for some freaking marathon at the same time?!"

The panting-filled run was almost over as the boy slowed down his pace and noticed a phone call was interrupting his audiobook listen. He answered and took a few deep breaths to catch enough air to talk, "Hello?" It was his mother. Calling, as she sometimes did, she wanted to learn how her son was doing, what had been the outcome of the recent work-related drama, and when he was going to confirm coming back home for Christmas. "Hi sweetheart, how are you feeling today?" she started. "I'm okay, Mom, just finishing my run as you can probably hear," he struggled to sift the words through the heavy breathing. "How are things with your work colleague?" she asked, "did you make peace after last week?" It was obvious she would be asking about it, the boy thought, "Yes, I mean, I think it's okay..." "Not much I can do, you know," he added, "I don't really think she likes or respects me much..." "Yes, I agree, of course, sometimes people just need a break," the girl continued, "but I don't think he cares about this project of ours at all..." "I know," she nodded, pacing around the living room, "I know, I need to try and understand him..." "It's okay," he tried to make a smile as his breathing finally relaxed, "I think we'll get on fine; it just takes time to accept and understand one another..." "Just make sure you see her point of view as well," his mom concluded, "I am sure she's a nice girl, maybe just doesn't understand how you do things, you know..." "Yes, yes, you're right, of course," he agreed, punching the code on the panel, "...alright, I'm going in, thanks for calling mom, I'll keep that in mind; love you!" He disconnected and walked towards the elevator.

"I mean, I am sure he is trying to make the most of it too," she felt a little less tense, "he does quite a bit, and if that's what helps him; yes, I know, I know..." She heard the elevator ding outside the flat. "Alright, let's switch topics okay," she said quietly into the phone, "I think he's back; I will try to understand him, I promise."

The door opened. The two went about their evening as usual, exchanged a few pleasantries, and wished each other good night. For their success as a team, in this unusual setting of working and living with your workmate, they found themselves in, they had to understand and accept one another. It was a matter of making or breaking it all. Certainly, neither of them wanted to break the project completely. So, out of necessity, they tried to make the effort. They tried to see the other's point of view as if it was their own. It didn't instantaneously make them friends, and most likely was not going to make them friends anytime soon, but at least the arguing and animosity subsided. They came to a silent, never verbalized agreement that whatever the other was doing, one would not assume the motive, rather reflect on the solution.

"It is not about how you appear to others," his mom said that night, "that's their business... It's all about what you do that makes you who you are." "Show them what you're made of, be patient, and do your best to understand them," she added, "everything else will come along."

Chapter 6. Live and Let Live

Now, this chapter may not be something you would expect since what we talked about so far was rather light-hearted and easy-going, but I am afraid it is necessary to touch on this topic before we go any further. There are a few reasons why I want you to reflect on this phrase here, right now, one of them being – we are surrounded by others. It's just a fact. In our day and age, only a few decide to leave the 'civilized' world behind and find their space somewhere in the quiet of the forest or the desert, and even those are rarely completely alone. People are all over the world and love to travel, so even in your solitary hut in the mountains, you are likely to bump into someone from time to time. So, yes, learning how to live with one another is a big and important thing to consider. When it comes to our choices and preferences, there is no individual in the world whose opinion will match another's with 100% accuracy. It's just impossible. With all the different backgrounds, experiences, and perspectives 'under our belts,' we are all unique and so complex, we are more likely to be very different from many, than have many things in common with a few. The beauty of ourselves is often in those differences we have, but we need not acknowledge them as qualities in themselves if this perception was to lead us to believe we are somewhat better than anyone else. Everyone is different and everyone is unique but let us not forget the most important aspect of being alive – everyone is blessed with this same ability and so we need to respect that above anything else.

In the previous chapters, we've touched on the topic of self-expression, self-understanding, and living with a purpose, which is often manifested in our intuitive choices and desires. Now, with all that knowledge gathered, we need to recognize the importance of allowing everyone else to choose and follow their own path. This means, noticing that the needs, wants, and passions of those around us are as valid to them as ours are to us, and giving a silent blessing to their nature without trying to change it or judge it in any way. It is not our place to do so. Just live and let live.

Throughout your life, you will come to live next to and often with many people, at least hundreds of thousands of them, to be more exact. You will have a chance to meet people at your university dorms, company offices, in restaurants, cafés, and in many other places where people come to enjoy themselves from time to time. You may travel the world, see new places, meet different cultures, and bask in the glory of the variety our world has to offer. It is a true blessing to be alive and quite an adventure to enjoy. But as we go about our days, minding our own business, we need to be aware of our own tendency to judge and impose our beliefs, wants, and needs onto everyone and anything around us. This affliction is a part of ourselves and will likely stay with us for the most part of our lives, so instead of fighting with its origins, we need to acknowledge it and train 'not to care.' This may sound like I want you to stop yourself from observing and judging what is going on around you in terms of your own perspective. Not at all! Being observant and able to judge the outcomes and situations that occur is an important aspect of learning how to act more skilfully and enjoy this journey called life even more. But judging should stop at that – judging within. From a practical standpoint, by considering the outcome of a certain situation, you can learn from it and let it influence your skills of living. The moment you start judging the person or their attitudes, especially in a negative manner, you lose the point and make a huge mistake. By letting emotions take part in the judgment, you are no longer aware of what you're perceiving. Live and let live. Observe and see what is going on. Experience and reflect on your experiences. Acknowledge and strengthen your wisdom with the knowing noticed. But do not judge and impose your own point of view on anyone else. Never. For your own sake, never allow yourself to do that.

There are two reasons why I strongly recommend you put this phrase into practice and consider it often. Firstly, your subjective perspective is likely to be far off point and most likely flawed, since you are unable to know every single detail about the person and their life's situation, which may have caused them to act in a certain way. By jumping to conclusions and deciding that you are better than them because you wouldn't do this or that, you are simply closing yourself off from the lessons and riches of the insight the situation has to offer. Instead of being receptive to it all, you close your mind. Instead of staying actively engaged with life, you fall into the deep sleep of unconscious biases and judgmentalism. And, as I mentioned five verses earlier, you are probably wrong anyway.

Secondly, by any means of imposing your perspective or attitude on others, you are likely to make them angry and defensive but will not change their mind. Changing minds does not happen externally. It is a process that each person needs to participate in on their own, within. If a person is not open to learn a new thing, they will struggle with it more than someone who feels like learning this activity is their must or want. It is like walking through a door. For you to walk through the door of their mind freely, they have to open it for you. No use jamming yourself right in there because by the time you crack it open, they have probably vacated the space. Who wouldn't? After all, someone was trying to break into their comfort zone. That's how imposing our opinions and ways on others could be represented. It is an intrusive and ineffective act. You are more likely to make them angry, lose their friendship, and cause yourself some trouble than if you were to say nothing and… yes, you guessed it – live and let live.

It is important to acknowledge that what we want for ourselves and hold dear to our hearts, others probably cherish too. One of these things, one of the most important ones, is just this – the freedom of choice. Everyone wants to be able to live as they please, and until choosing to make a change, they should be allowed to stay the same, as long as they do not hurt anyone or anything with their way of being. So, as we continue this adventure and dive deeper into the subjective patterns and miracles of our life, remember to live and let live. Allow others to be who they are because that is what makes them so special.

Live and let live.

'Imagine where you will be, and it will be so…'

~ Maximus in *Gladiator*

Story 7.

"You may wish for these things of yours all you want, but unless you take action, you're going to keep wishing," his father told him as they got out of the car and walked towards the door. "It always depends on what you do, not what you want." Upon stepping inside, the boy ran up the stairs to his room without a word. He was annoyed at his dad. "What the hell does he know?" he thought. They went to visit a few schools he was interested in joining, but as they discussed the things necessary for the boy to get accepted into either of them, his father tried to explain why taking additional classes may help. He didn't like that. "I don't need any special treatment," he barked back in the car, "of course, I will get into one of them with my grades!" As much as he might have been right, his parent attempted to reason with this pride and certainty by explaining that with the education sector being more and more saturated, the competition will rise and make things more difficult for the upcoming students. "It's up to you, of course," his father pointed out, "you don't have to do what I'm telling you to do, but, as I care about you and your success, I am trying to make you understand that your plan may work, or it may not..." "But there are ways of making sure you raise your chances," he added, "that's all."

Sitting in his room with a frown-filled face, he shrugged his shoulders again and again, as if shuffling off an uncomfortable shawl. He was quite good at school. His grades were not the worst, most of them hanging around the higher third of the class. His preparations for the exam were going okay, and he was participating in many volunteering activities, which gave him additional few points towards the final count. In other words, he was a slightly above-average student. And the schools which he decided to apply for were also, in his view and according to the last year's statistics, slightly above average. "Perfect for me," he announced a few days earlier. Struggling to accept the whole situation and the proposition mentioned by his caregiver, he twisted and turned in the uncomfortable silence of his room. He knew that whatever his father was saying was said in his best interest, and that frustrated him even more. Even though he didn't want to admit it, his father was likely to be right. He usually was. "Damn," he murmured, "additional classes, really?"

After some time had passed, the boy peeked out of the room, listened in, estimated that downstairs was clear due to the lack of any noises, and decided to get something to eat from the kitchen. There was no one in the living room, but upon entering the kitchen, he bumped into his father making himself some tea and checking business news for the week. He glanced at him without a word. The boy didn't say anything either. He grabbed a slice of bread, toasted it in silence, which made him feel uncomfortable, and made himself a simple peanut butter jelly sandwich. He could feel his father observing him from the table as he finished preparing the snack. "You know I want the best for you, son," his father started. Silence. "There is nothing more than I want for you but the best," he continued, "and whatever that may be, in your opinion, I shall agree upon it, as long as it does not jeopardize your health, wellbeing, and success in being all you could be." Silence. The boy moved slightly, turned around, and looked at him without a word. "All I am saying is, that if you want to get something, be something, or do something, you have to make some sacrifices."

Later that day, the boy was walking the dog, thinking about the whole subject of having what he wants to have, being who he wants to become, and doing what he wishes to do. It was not an easy topic to ponder. First of all, it was rather impossible to see it all at once and plan it out, as the world was too complex to simply anticipate it all. Secondly, he felt that by adding more responsibilities to his day, he was going to miss out on spending time with his friends and lose a part of his adolescent life. Moreover, it felt like a strain on his pride, which at the time was at its height since his sense of self was being developed. "What does he know?" he argued. Following the dog, he noticed that from time to time it was the dog walking him, rather than him walking the dog. It was as if the animal would follow a scent and change direction, and if the boy was not attentive and stern, they would go a different way than planned by him. He observed that for some time before drawing a little conclusion. "Maybe that's what it is," he thought, "maybe by making choices we aim at a certain goal, but then we have to pay attention and adjust the course accordingly." He went back home, researched the standards, and expected the level of proficiency needed for each of the schools he wished to attend, and thought whether his above-average performance was likely to allow him to get there without a hiccup. "I guess not necessarily," he heard the inner answer.

"Alright, Dad, I shall do it," he announced in the evening, during dinner, "I'll pick up a few additional classes from the most important subjects, so I can make sure I get to that school I wish to go to." He awaited a response, as his parents exchanged looks and smiled slightly. "What made you change your mind?" his mother asked. "Ehh... I do not want to miss out on seeing my friends, that's *true, but not attending a few meetings is not as painful as failing to get into the school I'd like to attend for the next three years,"* he *answered without looking at them, "it's worth the effort, and I understand that. And once I'm there, I can come back to seeing my friends more often for the next three years again... It's a sacrifice I am willing to make."*

Chapter 7. Make a Wish

With the understanding and acknowledgment of others ready to be employed, you are better prepared to truly dive into what this wonderful life of yours can offer. We should always clean up our rooms before we tell others off for not keeping theirs clean. So, by doing the inner work you've attempted in the earlier chapters, you can freely join life's flow, knowing you're doing your best with a clear conscience.

This time, we will finally make those wishes we've considered earlier. You know what you like, you are aware of what's not necessarily your cup of tea, and you should know, by now, where this could lead you. Life is a journey, so expect many twists and turns. You need to know where you're going, even if you have no clue just yet how to get there. That's just how it works sometimes. Thinking of the wishes and desires you listed, the things you appreciate doing and surrounding yourself with, choose one and write it here.

[WRITE HERE]

It need not be a big one. Any of your wishes is good enough for us to start with. As you grow more confident in yourself and the process we're embarking on, you can use the following steps to move towards all of the wishes and needs you feel like pursuing. The mechanism of this is very simple, but the effort and adventure that come with it may feel hard at times, which is why it is best to start small. In order to better explain this to you, I have chosen a simple example: that of writing my first book back in 2020/21 called '(Un)usual Stories'. I know what you are thinking: 'Writing a book is not something I'm interested in.' Fair enough, but there certainly is a different goal, whether material or conceptual in nature, which you would find interesting and worthy of pursuit. Don't you agree?

Anyway, notice the steps in the process which I have gone through, and you will know the secret (which won't be that much of a secret, once I share it with you) to getting what you wish for. First, I've had to make a choice of what I wanted to pursue. In my situation, it was writing a book. I decided it didn't have to be perfect, but I wanted it to be of certain quality and raise a particular set of ideas. I then researched the available guidance 'on writing', including reading books such as Stephen King's 'On Writing: A Memoir Of The Craft', and explored some techniques which may have been of use to my goal's favour. With the details in place, I did the necessary maths, understood how much time it would take me to write the stories I've envisioned, and what it would take to put them all together. Then, I've looked over the writings I have committed to date and reviewed this sketch of a plan once more. What is more, I've scheduled regular writing reviews every two weeks, to help me stay on course, recognize whether I am heading in the right direction, and see where I could improve my performance rate or loosen up a little. It did not take me longer than an hour each two weeks to do those 'check-ins', and after a year or so, I have succeeded in cataloguing a fair number of stories suitable for this vision of mine. Of course, I had to put in the hours in front of the page, face the music of my inner critic a number of times, and had fallen behind with my project from time to time, but overall, it was rather easy and even pleasant, especially knowing that the achievement would be completely mine.

Okay, have you noticed the few steps I mentioned earlier? How many are there? Take a moment now and read through this brief story again. Write down below a number of steps you believe were needed and try to recognize what each of them is. I will give you a few minutes to do this. Do not turn the page before you are ready! Learning demands of us to think, not to merely follow. So think now! Think and find exactly what made my success possible. Good luck!

[WRITE HERE]

Alright, how did that go? Did you find them?! I bet you've found at least a few of them. It's not that hard to see them after all. Most of us use these steps every day with almost everything we do. It's just that sometimes we do not know exactly why we do what we do because it is not necessary to know in order to do these things. Reflecting on such dynamics can be a great way of becoming more aware of ourselves, our patterns of behaviours, and our ideas of the world. For now, we will focus on these steps, but later in the book, I promise to come back to this phenomenon and help you understand your own patterns a little more. Ready?

So, when it comes to the story about the book, there were five major steps, which helped me create the opportunity for myself and achieve the wished-for outcome. First of all, I made a decision (a choice) about my goal. The goal was the book. I made sure to express all the details of it and considered the three questions – what, when, and why. The third question is particularly powerful, as it adds the emotion (the flavour) to your goal. It was Nietzsche who stated, "he who has a why can bear almost any how". These are some powerful words, and I would like you to remember them. Okay, so the decision and its description were our number one. What was the second step? Once the goal is chosen, we need to come up with a plan of how to get to that goal. It doesn't mean you have to know it all already. If you're like me or most of the world, you'll probably have a few ideas on possible ways, but not much of a plan, especially if what you are aiming for is very new to you. Regardless of these details, you should write down as many ideas as you can come up with and decide which ones seem the most likely to work. To start, you only need one or two steps planned, so do not get too worried if your plan doesn't explain the whole journey. You need to plan what you can do right here, right now, because that is where you are. It is when you start. At this stage, I had a rough idea of what it would take to write and compile a book full of stories and realized the commitments I would have to decide on. Small and simple steps are the best ones.

The third part is where many people fail. There is a saying, "try and fail, but do not fail to try…" Another to add to your collection, as you prepare for your next adventure. This step is very important, maybe even the most important of them all, because without it, you will not get anywhere further than the paper in front of you. You need to TAKE ACTION. You have to make that first step. It may sound too simple to be true, but it is true. Whatever we may wish to do, be, or have, we must take a step towards it to make it a part of our life. Your bestselling book won't write itself. Your dream car won't just appear outside your flat. The love of your life won't fall down the sky on you on one of those sunny days. It is up to us to move towards these things when we decide to ask for them. We have to take responsibility for starting the process. Do not worry too much about the next step for now, just do the first one! In my situation, it was about creating a space and time for myself to do the heavy lifting of actually writing. Yes, you heard me, actually writing. As simple as that. I took action, which helped in continuing the journey. And so you have to do that too. "Every great adventure starts with a single step," a wise person once stated. Remember that. Take the first step. Take action.

Okay, so by now, you may realize what I will invite you to do next. If you're already on your way, you have an idea of a plan (at least for the next day) and you know plenty about your goal, it is time to review what is going on. Like a rocket staying on course to the moon, you need to keep control of your direction. Notice that it is rather impossible to know if you're heading in the right direction if you do not know where you want to go. That is why choosing the goal is so important. As you continue on your journey, you will find moments of being lost as well as moments of knowing where to go. It is all a part of the process. Trust it. Continue. Keep at it. Keep reviewing your directions. In my situation, it was all about checking my writing habits and progress. Every two weeks, I would sit down and summarize my performance, thinking of ways to improve it or slow down if I had to. You need to keep this strategy in mind and use it regularly. Wherever you are going, these reflection moments will give you three great gifts. You will know if you're heading in the right direction, you will be able to recognize what needs to change, and you will see your progress happening, which is a beautiful and highly inspiring experience. It will keep your head in the game. It will keep you motivated. So, with the goal in mind, with the plan in place, and with actions taken, you have to keep the course. You have to stay on top of your game. You have to revise.

Finally, the fifth step is so simple it needs no repeating. It's repetition. Yes, I know you like what I just did there (ha ha). The last piece of the puzzle becomes the first one, and the first one becomes the last one whenever you make advances towards your goal. It is all about continuing the journey. A beautiful quote I've heard somewhere stated that "consistency beats talent every day". Of course, I don't think you need to perceive other people with their goals as your competition, but it can be useful to see yourself as competition to yourself. After all, there are many kinds of people inside you, aren't there? Sometimes you feel lazy, sometimes motivated. Sometimes everything is going great, and sometimes you don't know what is happening. It is normal for each of us to feel this way. That is why it is so important to recognize that whatever talents you may have, it is the persistence, disciplined effort, and consistency of action that makes the real difference. You are in charge of your time and your time only. Do not waste it doing what you know you shouldn't. Just think of how difficult writing a book in a week may sound and how easy it can seem when you decide to write one page a day. This is how I've written this book. One page at a time. Morning after morning. Choosing to do something every day, even if it only takes you five minutes to do it, is the best way of strengthening your discipline muscle and achieving great goals. It will feel less intense and more within your reach if you decide to approach your goal with this idea in mind. As you can see, achievement does not have to be overwhelming. There are ways to take action, which enable us to put big things into smaller pieces and succeed in doing them over time with much less stress. To run a marathon, you should probably first run a mile.

To help you remember these steps I've created this anagram – S.P.A.R.K. You have to (S)ee your goal, (P)lan it as much as you can, (A)ct to create movement, (R)eview to continue in the right direction, and (K)eep going. By putting these steps in place, you will certainly get closer to your goals, whatever they may be. Just like a muscle, your discipline needs to be trained.

And it all starts with the first step – making a wish…

'Fashions fade, style is eternal.'

~ Yves Saint Laurent

Story 8.

There was always a slight sense of unease accompanying her as she went from one activity to another, especially when others were present. Even in the company of her friends and family, she did not feel completely at peace with the way her thoughts made her feel. There seemed to be something out of place, something missing. Like with most people in the world, the girl struggled with the feeling of not being good enough, whatever that may mean. She felt that her smile was not bright enough, her gaze lacked the spark needed to attract her prince charming, and her performance was often far from ideal. It didn't matter that pretty much everyone else also experienced shortcomings. As it usually happens, with the fixation and subjective perspective of oneself, she could only see her own faults and flaws when going about her day. It was that part of the human condition that caused her suffering.

Reflecting on these troubles one morning, she confided her worries and pains to her dearest friend, one whom she knew for as long as she could remember: Her best friend ever. "I do something and then I feel stupid, or I think of saying something and realize it would be crazy to do so," she explained shyly, "it's as if on one hand I feel like it's the right thing to do, while on the other it makes me worry what everyone would think..." Her friend hesitated before responding, as she herself also struggled with the same trouble. It was easy to advise others, but taking the same advice and applying it to oneself was something else. Recognizing this paradox, the girl thought of what would be best to say, "I feel the same way, you know...?" The answer surprised them both. It was helpful to hear such a statement and to speak it, as they felt the slight relief of a pain shared, like a heavy bag lifted by the two, instead of being carried around on one's shoulders. "Really?" *the girl asked with disbelief,* "how come, you're always so calm and smiling..." "I could say the same about you," *she answered. They looked at one another with their eyes wide open. They finally could see it. The paradox. The irony.* "That's funny..." "Do you think everyone else feels this way...?" *The question they both thought was finally vocalized and thinking about the answer, the two felt a bit more comfortable in their own skins.* "I mean, if it is the same for us two, chances are more people have this too," *one of them answered,* "it would make sense, wouldn't it...?" *A sense of relief allowed them to look at the topic with more reserve. At the very least, if no one ever felt as bad or uncertain as they did, they had one another to understand the pain. It was very helpful. Misery does like company, after all.*

They thought about these things, reflecting on the moments when one would feel awkward and the other would perceive them as confident and happy, and vice versa. It was obvious that what one was feeling, the other was rarely able to fully spot. "Why is that...?" *one of the girls finally jumped up with a demand for an answer in her tone,* "why do we not appear to others as we are feeling with ourselves...?" "Maybe because they are too busy with their own feelings and troubles to pay attention...," *the answer followed. It was yet another uneasy but probable solution to the puzzle, and the two felt slightly lighter with the use of such theory.* "But if no one actually cares about what we appear like because they are too bothered thinking of their own situation, doesn't that make the whole idea of worrying about our appearance a little silly...?", *the girls drew a conclusion with noticeable relief.* "Wouldn't it be better *then," started one of them, "to focus on being how we want to be, regardless of what others may think, because this way we will feel better with ourselves, and in turn feel less bad about what others may think about us…?"* Bingo!

Chapter 8. Love Your Style

Now, since we are well on our way toward making yourself a little calmer and flowing through life with more ease, I would like to invite you to explore the style with which you live each day. Everyone has their own sense of style in all areas of life, so to simplify it, we will only explore the parts that involve your way of being with yourself, with others, and with your time. I am certain you realize the importance of time, which is why I would like to help you make better choices in spending it. I will not give you any advice, rather propose some questions that can help you advise yourself in the process. Please bear in mind the wishes, hopes, and likes you've mentioned earlier, as they will come in handy when we dive deeper into this sphere of "self-style management."

Let's start with the most important part of this puzzle – yourself. Socrates invites us to 'know thyself,' which will be a great place to begin. What do you know about yourself? You know you're a human being, you have a name, you know where your parents live and who they are, you may know something about the history of your family or your country of origin, you probably know your age. What else is there to know? Think of it as if you needed to tell someone who doesn't know you (like myself) who .... (enter your name) is. Who are you? Below, you will find half of the page empty and arranged in a way that might be helpful for this task. Of course, as always, feel free to use your notebook or a different space to do this exercise if you feel like it. I will give you about ten minutes this time. Think who you are and write it all down. Tell me about yourself!

[WRITE HERE]

Okay, it looks like you've done your best at this time. Remember, it doesn't matter how much or how little you engage with these exercises. What is important is that you try and always try to do your best. Whatever your true best is, do it, and you'll be flying through your life like a superstar. So, you've written down some notes for me to read, which I will do later; most likely, once you leave this book on the side and go do something else. For now, I would like you to look at these things you've written again and think of your personal style. What do I mean by that...?! Oh, of course, let me explain.

Your personal style, in my opinion, is how you show up in the world. What do you represent? Who is .... (enter your name)? What do you do? People often introduce themselves with their work title, their marital status, or their astrological sign. All of that is okay, but I think there is more to us than what we do, who we are with, or which time of the year in the sky was present at the time of our birth. We are all so unique! Why don't we introduce ourselves based on these unique features? Look at the previous exercise once more and find one or two things, actions, or interests that really make you feel joyful and excited even as you think about them. What makes your heart jump up and down with love?

As I mentioned, it can be useful to look back at chapter 4. Whatever you choose, recognize your personal style in it. Whether you are a passionate dancer, you love post stamps, or get very excited about the new model of that amazing smartphone, these things, and your reaction to them have a big impact on the kind of person you try to be each day. You may not recognize it, but if you're into dancing, you may tend to do things rhythmically, listen to music a lot, and walk quite lightly wherever your legs take you. As a post stamp enthusiast, you are probably quite a meticulous and patient person with a keen eye for detail, since it doesn't only take quite an effort to find that collectible online, you also have to ensure your collection is neatly arranged and free from any injuries. A smartphone freak like yourself could also be into exploring new technology discoveries the world is constantly coming up with, is likely to get excited about ideas and new solutions all the time, and probably does not like to sit in one place for too long. Without going too much into the personality traits each of us has, this exercise is here to help you recognize and think of the style you have, thanks to how you are. Take a moment now and write down some loose ideas of how what you love to do, be, or have makes you act.

To help you, here is an exemplary description of mine, which I came up with as I was thinking of this exercise for you: *I love to* write and travel. I like new ideas, talking with people, and adventures. I get bored easily, do not like too much routine, and often get impatient. I have a lot of energy and cannot stop thinking of the next exciting event that I will be participating in. I struggle to focus, but when I write, I get laser focused. Don't know why. I guess that's just my style. And if I were to represent my style in an image, I would come back to the story I've written a few years ago about a bear riding a unicycle, with a sloth on his back, juggling five balls, and balancing a sword on its nose. If you want to know the explanation, check this story out in my previous book, but don't worry too much about it. It's just my way of imagining how my style looks. That's all.

So, now you know what you need to do in the exercise. Write down a few aspects of yourself you can see emerging from the previous activities and consider what they could say about you. Think of how you would portray this array of characteristics and do not stop yourself from silly ideas. There are no bad ideas in the realm of the abstract. You can think whatever you wish to think. You can imagine whatever you manage to imagine. Your head, your rules! Remember that! Write your thoughts below and take at least five minutes mulling over this. Treat it as a fun exercise and do not stress about it too much. Allow yourself to really go crazy with this. Take your time; I'll wait.

[WRITE HERE]

Okay! That seems like a pretty outrageous portrayal of your style. I love it! I am very happy you've challenged yourself to try and approach this topic. Keep an open mind; we are just getting started.

As we've already discussed before, understanding ourselves is one of the most important steps in becoming better at whatever we are or want to be. It's close to impossible to solve a problem if you do not know what the problem is. Of course, you are no problem, but in terms of understanding yourself to make yourself feel better, happier, healthier, etc., knowing thyself will play a big role! You have to know where you are to know where to direct your next step! There is no use for a map without orienting it in space! Before we jump into the next black hole of funky tasks and self-adventures, I would like to point out the idea behind 'living and letting live' and how it adheres to this sense of style. As you may have already noticed, each of us will likely write down a different set of style-making components, and the mixture will look completely unique for each participant. That is what makes the world so interesting and talking with people so fascinating. We are all different. Very different. Yes, we do have similar interests sometimes. Yes, we do appreciate some mutual traditions when we come from the same area. And yes, we do often put sugar in our tea rather than a pinch of salt. There are many reasons to point out our similarities, and that's wonderful, but the truth of the matter is, most of these are still just surface layers of our beings. As long as you do not define yourself by the way you drink your tea, you are likely to be as complex and mostly mysterious as any other person in this world. What is most different in each of us is the way we think and act. Our attitude towards failure, our emotional tantrums, our laughter, and things that make this laughter come to life. All of these, and many more, are completely, utterly subjective. Even trying to explain ourselves, we struggle to truly grasp the essence of our style. That is why, with all due respect to anyone and everyone out there, I would invite you to recognize your style and the tone it gives you whenever you interact with others. Do not be too defensive about your way of being. It's great as it is, and you may want to keep it this way, but you need to recognize its soft spots to minimize the risk of getting on someone's nerve. No one deserves to be offended, so I would advise you to leave the negativity behind.

Looking at my example, I know that I often can come across as quite arrogant and impatient, even when I am trying my best to do something for another person. My style causes my tone of voice and facial expression to sour the heart of the other. Things happen. I cannot always stop myself from this, but at least I can notice it as a tendency and try my best in minimizing the collateral. Before we go further, take a moment to consider what characteristics of your way of being, of your style, could potentially cause suffering or unpleasant feelings in another. Recognize them for what they are – your quirks, tiny spots on the clean slate of your person, your unique features. Accept them and love them, but do not allow them to drive too often. They can cause you a lot of trouble if you let them loose around the block. Take them for what they are, consider their potential influence on others, and get into the practice of noticing them when their nasty little heads show up on the surface of your stylish coat. It often happens that the very extreme of our strength is prone to hurt others if used without thinking about it and acting skilfully.

Finally, remember that these spots and unique flaws are part and parcel of everyone's life, so try to go easy on people around you as you notice their tiny gnomes showing up. Share empathy with others and share empathy with yourself. Do your best, respect everyone, and love yourself for what you are.
Love your style.

'If you're going to try, go all the way…'
~ Charles Bukowski

Story 9.

"You always have to have everything planned out, analysed, blueprinted, and sketched out to the tiniest detail," she pointed out with obvious irritation. *"Don't you think for one moment, that by making such ridiculous assumptions, you're not only killing the vibe of our plans, but you are also coming up with utter absurdities?!"* They were supposed to go for a holiday vacation, and as it usually happened between them, it was 'that time of the year' to argue about the plans during their time away once more. She always fancied spontaneous trips—a few ideas, putting them on a piece of paper, and just 'going with the flow' to explore and see where the journey takes them. For him, such an approach was borderline silliness. He wanted a firm plan, a good and efficient schedule, and a backup narrative, in case something would be closed or impossible to get to. Two different attitudes and two different people. Like in many love stories of this world, they were also together, so these differences, whatever they may have been, had to be addressed and worked with rather than abandoned or overlooked.

"It's best to have a plan, so we do not waste time," he argued. *"We only have two weeks of vacation, and I want us to make the most of it..."* *"We can make the most of it by living in the moment and actually enjoying it, instead of looking at the clock to 'be on time' for the next sightseeing visit,"* her voice was lowered but stern. *"What's the pleasure of exploring the city if you're doing it mid-sprint between the buildings...?"*

Both had a point, but they certainly held onto a different one. Thinking of this all in silence, the girl finished packing her bag and left the room. The boy sat at the desk, staring at the many lists, maps, and notes he prepared. He wanted the trip to be fun above all, and it seemed like, yet again, the fun was already evaporating, even before their flight was to take off. Suddenly, the sound of the front door closing strongly echoed across the hall. He knew she went out to walk and think. She always did that when they were having an argument. With his hand still squeezing the highlighter and hovering above the attraction list on the desk, he pondered the situation they were getting themselves into.

"What's so bad about all this planning?" he shrugged in slight irritation. "It certainly feels right to make the most of our time there..."

And then, as he reflected on this inconceivable for him but so obviously important aspect for his love, he remembered a situation from one of his trips before. He was walking around a seaside town in Southern Europe on one of the first days of his trip when he realized that the map and the list of attractions he wanted to see stayed behind in his hotel. He was already about forty minutes from the location and didn't feel like going back would be worth it. It was on that day that he actually got to see some truly impressive and completely unexpected aspects of the city. Without a map, he was more inclined to ask for directions, which allowed him to meet one of his friends, and because he had no longer a plan for where to go, he ended up spending much more time in the spontaneous search of adventure, which was quite an interesting experience. Of course, the next day, with his map and list ready, he went around ticking the boxes off, and so he forgot much about that one-day hiccup, but thinking about it now, he realized the uniqueness and value of that situation. He understood what his girlfriend wanted them to do. It was then when he decided to leave the plans in the side pocket of his backpack, but only as a reserve of ideas, in case they would need some inspiration. Then, he picked up the phone, called her, and explained the new plan. "Sometimes the best plan is no plan at all," he concluded.

Chapter 9. Don't think, just go.

Much could be said about the philosophy of thinking. We often think so much we don't do anything else but that. Thinking so long, hard, deep, and thoughtfully, we don't have time for doing anything else. Much could be said about it, and most likely you've heard it all already. There are schools of thought, discussion groups, brainstorming sessions, think tanks, dinner-table considerations, and paper-based thoughts—plenty of them to choose from, quite frankly, a little too many.

Although I have nothing against these entities of a sort, as I can appreciate their immense potential to inspire, empower, and uplift us to higher states of mind, body, or soul, I also recognize the trouble they often cause to people like me and you when the time to act comes. I know you know that I know what I am talking about. I bet you are aware of this phenomenon in your life, and I may be right when I say you would prefer, I leave this stone unturned. Well, sorry, my book, my rules. You can come along with me on this adventure or simply put it down. No biggie. Your call.

Thinking and analysing everything has become a way of keeping ourselves in the comfort zone 'for just a little longer'. It's a safety net with which many of us strangle our dreams and plans. It is a way of saying, 'I am going to do that, but I just need a few more minutes to figure out the best approach; best technique; best time; best whatever'. Let's be honest, all of us do it. We allow this 'thinking trend' to stop us from applying for that competition, inviting that guy out, taking out the novel from the drawer and sending it to the publisher, going to the gym for the first time, etc.

We give it a free pass to stop us in the starting position for a tad longer. Short enough to feel like we're about to 'go for it' and long enough to secretly untie our laces and pull our shorts halfway down. Like a comforting blanket of snow, it may feel cosy at the beginning, but if you stay underneath long enough it won't let you go any further.

Let me make this clear. It is not the think tank or the thought process itself that I deem to be bad. As Shakespeare wrote, 'nothing is good or bad but thinking makes it so'. So, let's not blame our indolence on anything or anyone other than ourselves. I don't have anything against them. Quite frankly, I believe them to be great and empowering mediums of knowledge transfer and creativity enhancers. It's not about them per se, but the use of them by us. By you and me. In the same way we've been trying to decipher the ways we act (with style) in this realm of existence; we must decode the ways we sabotage our efforts or excuse ourselves from stalling the engine of our success.

Think about it! How many times did you hesitate before starting something new or trying for your wish in a sudden surge of enthusiasm? If you're anything like me, you hesitate most of the time. We all do. It's no surprise if you consider the millennia of survival our species had to endure to get us where we are right at this moment. Although there are barely any tigers threatening our lives today (more like we are threatening them…), our survival mechanism is still present and going strong. Thanks to it, we are able to cope with the stresses of life and avoid being hit by a car, but for the most part, it makes us think twice about every little, tiniest potentially stressful thing, activity, or event we could imagine. Its name is fear, and it has many faces, one of which is the one we're considering in this chapter – overthinking. I quite like how 'overthinking' reminds me of the end this type of thinking offers. Making it all 'over', overthinking provides us with the right number of thoughts, worries, and hesitations to kill the plan, project, or idea in its very womb. Straight and to the point. Quick snip. No pain, no gain—just this time with an ironic loss on our side.

We are so good at "thinking things over" and "overthinking things" that most of our waking life belongs to either of the two. The first one, in my opinion, refers to considerations and reconsiderations we grant to our past experiences. "We think things over and over," trying to digest their happening and the many pros and cons our behaviour at "that time" presented. Let us not forget, it is a great way of staying in one place, of course, as you cannot really go forward efficiently while you are looking back in constant reflection. It is a pull into the past, which no longer exists. The second approach feels more familiar to me and is similarly hindering. "Overthinking things" allows us to look far into the future, much further than our immediate surroundings ever could, and by pondering the potential directions in which we would be heading those lightyears later, we hesitate to make the next step here and now. I like to portray it to myself as a hesitant pedestrian, whose gaze is fixed on the other side of the bridge, paralyzed by the worries of approaching the castle, while he's still standing in the mud down the hill. I know, sounds quite radical and confusing. It is like so for a reason. This kind of thinking allows us to be so overly concerned about the next few years, we forget to make the most of today. It's a pull into the future, which will never come.

Before you start coming up with reasons why we look back or look forward on the daily basis, let me admit that there are benefits to both of these approaches. Of course, by reflecting on the past we can recognize our weaknesses and strengths. It can also help us understand our situation better and appreciate the path we have travelled to get where we are today. That's all fair and square. Similarly, planning can save us some precious time and help us choose more wisely. It can inform us about the wishes and expectations we have for the upcoming days, weeks, months, or years, and support our skilful navigation of this lively vessel of ours. If you consider yourself and your health in ten years, you will be more likely to avoid the many substances and activities that may compromise this healthy future of yours here and now. Looking forward can be a great tool for navigation. But, yet again, it should be just that—a tool.

My invitation in this chapter does not dismiss the idea that both modes of thinking have their advantages. That's certain and I do agree. Instead, I am sharing with you these words copied off the paper of my mind to yours because I want you to beware of glorifying the process of thinking as a value in and of itself. It is a tool, not a destination. You can use it, or it can use you. As simple as that. Having this in mind, I am going to challenge you, as well as myself, since I am the first person to read and engage with this book in any way, to reflect on the things or activities you've been postponing with the help of these lovely "thoughtful fellows" and choose three that you will not postpone anymore. Promise me and yourself to act upon them. Make the first step. Get out of the mud, approach the street, cross it safely, and start climbing up towards the castle. Take that hill. Do the deed. Act.

Without a doubt, we live in times of information overload. On every screen, corner of the street, and even a stranger's T-shirt, we are "informed" of something, and rarely these "nuggets of insight" are worth much more than a used tissue. The world screams to hijack our attention and draws it in directions that are far from positive or empowering. Most of it is just crap. Your attention and brain can only take so much of it before it lowers down its guard and allows the punches of messaging to shake its core. We will come back to this topic in more detail, but for now, I want you to put into practice the five-second rule. No matter how good you are at counting seconds, just count to five, and you'll be fine. I want you to use it whenever you're feeling the arising hesitation considering the past or the future. Whenever you're thinking about doing something, consider it for no more than five seconds, and as long as it won't put you or anyone else in harm's way, do it. Allow the "counting to five" method to inspire and empower you. Whatever you think about, you may think what you want, but I want you to DO SOMETHING ABOUT IT.

Don't think, just go!

'Freedom comes from strength and self-reliance.'
~ Lisa Murkowski

Story 10.

Their walk up the hill was becoming more difficult with each step. Both had backpacks to carry, containing the necessities needed for a few days' worth of adventure in nature, and each carried a few items in their hands as well. It was not an easy task, but as striving for success usually is, it was a task worth the effort. The two were brothers, one slightly younger than the other. They were enjoying a summer weekend getaway and decided to spend some time together hiking around the local hills and valleys. Since both of them were already adults, they didn't have much time to spend together on a daily basis. Moreover, they lived away from each other, as one of the brothers chose to move cities for the job he acquired, which made meetings even more of a hassle. Dragging the things up, the two huffed and puffed quietly, each staring at the rocky path beneath his feet. They were not able to talk at that moment. The older brother was leading the way, as they emerged between two big rocks into a clearing of the valley. The sun was high, making them squint as they looked up and measured the way still to go.

"Let's take a break," said one of them. The other nodded and sat down where he stood. It was more of a fall than a sit down if you consider the velocity with which his backpack-weighted body neared the ground. The younger brother took out a bottle of water and took a few sips before passing it on. They sat there, observing their surroundings in silence for a few moments. The sounds of nature and their attempts to catch their breath were the only audible noises in the area.

"Pretty, eh...?" one summed up finally. "Crazy that some people find this kind of activity futile, don't you think...?" the younger one finally spoke, turning the gaze to meet his fellow. "Yeah," the older brother acknowledged without much thought, "I guess they just don't see the fun part... maybe they never tried."

They sat there for some time without talking. The views were breath-taking, but these were but the beginning, and the two knew it well. They used to go on many such excursions back when they were younger. Their parents would take them for hikes across the mountains in the south or camping trips along the northern coast. It was a part of their summer holidays almost every year. Of course, at the time, it was not necessarily always what they wanted. One remembered the time when, because of his friends wanting to go abroad, he struggled to accept the family vacation offer. The other had a situation in which, due to his girlfriend's plans, he literally ran away a day before the trip to avoid missing out on going with his love. By now, they were able to laugh about it, but at the time it was nothing funny. Nothing funny at all.

The two were considering these things as they observed their surroundings. Now, older and with more responsibilities than ever, these trips from the past suddenly felt much more valuable than they ever thought them to be. They were the chances to build character, connect with the family, make great memories, and have fun. They were the moments to remember. And the two definitely did.

"I used to hate that old backpack I had to carry for three summers in a row," the older one said, as if knowing what the other was

thinking about, "it was so heavy and uncomfortable..." They chuckled. "Do you remember when Dad forgot the gas stove and we had to go all the way back through that forest one time?" the younger answered, "That was just crazy. Madness." His sibling nodded, "Madness." "It was fun though," he added, "if you think about it, it was really fun... And the views." "Yes, the views..."

Reminiscing, they fell silent again. "You know," one started, "I never told Mom about it, but I think that our summer trips really helped me with overcoming challenges later in life..." "They taught us resilience," his brother answered thoughtfully, "they knew what they were doing." "Yes," the younger followed, "I guess they really did..."

Pushing himself up, the older brother got up and raised his hands, as if to allow the backpack's arms to settle on his shoulders. "Alright, I think we should get going," he looked at his companion, "as Dad used to say, we better start walking before we realize the weight of the backpack..." They laughed and the other one got up. "Yeah, and don't look too far on the map, remember," he added, "because all that comes from thinking too much of the road ahead is a headache and disheartening..."

They continued on their journey, each in their own mind mulling over the past experiences and memories of the beautiful time spent with their loved ones. It has been almost five years since their father died, and as much as they would want to leave the subject behind, it was part of the daily effort to understand and consider what their hero would do. This trip they decided upon was an expression of that, a way of commemorating and finding peace *again. They were taught from a young age that one day, they would be alone. Everyone is, from time to time. That is how the world works. Even with friends and family by one's side, everyone sleeps alone at the end of the day. "That's why it is important you find and foster your own strength first," their father used to say, "because whatever may happen in the future, you will be in charge of your life..." "There are places where even your brother won't be able to come along," he would often add.*

Of course, as they grew older and more experienced, they started to understand these lessons better. The friends that once seemed so close and almost essential to one's happiness were mostly gone. The true friendships were always there, but with everyone living their own life, they were also just an addition, not the main dish. Their loved ones became their pivotal life's area. Their families were most important now. They were no longer going only for themselves; they were going for those they cared for as well. But the truth of the matter still stood, that their efforts, however collaborative they may be, were ultimately down to themselves. Each to their own. The two brothers knew this very well, and the backpacks they carried were the reminder of this truth. "Wherever you may go, whatever you may do, at the end of the day, you are responsible for yourself, and you need to carry your baggage of experiences alone," their mother once stated while recollecting one of the beautiful trips they had done with the whole family. "We are so proud of you both," she added, "you cannot even imagine how much..."

Chapter 10. Time To Get Real

It would not be fair for me to say that becoming more mindful, calmer, and more satisfied with what you do, be, and have in your life is easy. Quite frankly, it may just be one of the most challenging things you will face during your lifespan. That is for two reasons, of course. Firstly, it is not a one-time battle but a never-ending, daily toil because as you go through your days, weeks, and months, you will find that many situations will dare you to fall bitter and disheartened again and again. Secondly, there is no one that can help you in this, at least not in the essential, front-to-end, deep kind of way. Yes, you can get support from your loved ones, your friends, your psychiatrists, or your role models. Everyone will be able to give you a good piece of advice, to point you in the 'better' direction, to ask you 'how you're doing', bringing your awareness to the fact that these daily take-aways may not be the greatest option for your health, but ultimately the challenge of becoming a better version of yourself (whatever that may mean to you) is yours to take on and complete. It is your time, your life, and your homework.

I do not want to dismiss the idea that supportive communities help us tackle our demons and face the proverbial music of our daily struggles. Of course, they do. The thing is, however, that at the end of the day, 'we all sleep alone'. Your inner harmony is between you and you. No one else will ever be able to just come into your mind, your body, or your soul, and reorganize it. No one can make it sparkle more than it already does. No one, but you. You are 'the captain of your ship and the master of your soul'[1]. You have the power to change your ways. You have all the power you need, right here, right now.

Often, when people delve into these kinds of topics, the atmosphere somehow lowers its vibration. As if talking about challenges and self-care was too hard to handle, too much of morbid subjects to consider. As much as I appreciate that for some these subjects may seem a little overwhelming, I do not think there is much to them that should scare us from the consideration itself. Turning our gaze away from the fire does not stop it from burning the house to the ground, right? Dramatic? Maybe. Essential to our existence? Certainly.

The times we live in are unique because of the many improvements technology and connectedness across the globe have offered to our species. We came up with solutions to many immediate problems, making life easier and much more efficient than ever before. One click, and you have it. One swipe, and they like you. One flight, and you're gazing at the magnificent landscape halfway across the globe. Isn't it marvellous? Of course, these unique opportunities and improvements that life on Earth consists of these days are close to miraculous and certainly they do feel as if living became much more bearable, fun, exciting, and impressive. The problem, however, following the thought of a great thinker from the past is this: 'the world marches onward, but humans stay the same.' Our rate of adaptation does not match this accelerating technological world. We are creating solutions, which sound logical and provide

---

[1] *Invictus* by William Ernest Henley

much adored wonders, but do not consider the side effects their presence and utility may have on our levels of connectedness, satisfaction, and calm on a more humane, down-to-earth plane. We have come to be connected to the whole world but disconnected ourselves from our very own core. That is where the challenge lies, and that's where you may only help yourself. Everyone, even the closest of your loved ones, will have to stay outside as you dive deeper into the lovely, most likely a little dusty, inner world of yours.

And no, before you assume my point, I do not want to scare or demotivate you. Quite the opposite, to be honest. I want to empower you by making you realize the importance and power that lies within your own self. Regardless of what is going on in the outside world, we are blessed to have a choice of HOW we react to that world, and this is a superpower you can employ at any point in time! You are the master of your own inner world. We will come back to the trickiness of connectedness later in this book, but for now, remember this: you are in charge of yourself, and no one else, however hard they may try, will be able to change your perspective unless you allow them to. There are a few things you cannot delegate, and self-development and inner work are two of them we want to focus on for now. Think of it this way—if these cannot be influenced by anyone but yourself, don't they feel quite personal; don't they feel quite real? For me, working on myself, with myself, for myself, has been the most beautiful adventure so far. I see it as both a selfish and selfless act, considering I am the one who must spend time with me for the most part, but others and the world have to deal with me as well, even if I were to live a completely solitary existence. It is our nature to interact with the environment around us, and even in the loneliest of places in the world, I would have to be a partner to some solemn cave, a few branches, and a flint. What would they think of me and our acquaintanceship?

So, if you feel that self-care sounds like a selfish idea, consider the quality of the company you will present to your family and friends when you come into the room smiling and light-hearted versus what they would have to deal with if your appearance dragged along a stormy cloud of despair. Your wellbeing truly affects those around you. It's a fact. A great example of this kind of dynamic is the idea of an 'energy-draining vampire of a person'. I know, sounds spooky, but bear with me. Think for a moment about a time when, after meeting someone, for whatever reason, you felt quite deflated; like your energy has been drained; tired and somewhat sluggish. Can you remember such a scene? To make a point and contrast this feeling, think now about the person you feel so excited to see and spend time with that you literally burst with energy at the mere thought of it. They are the ones that fill you up so much you want to explode. You're almost flying when you're with them. Have you found their image? Easy, right?

That contrast is exactly what I mean when I say, consider your wellbeing as an essential part of the wellbeing of others. Would you rather be the energy drainer or the energizer? I know what I would choose. Making an effort to take care of ourselves serves more people than we may realize, and in the long run, by becoming a beacon of positivity and self-love, you grant permission and invitation to others that have the chance to experience your vibe to act in a self-appreciative manner too. Like a candle sharing its flame with another, you are able to light up the whole room. So, be brave in your inner work, trust your effort will bring forth the blessings of this world, and do not forget that it is between you and You. All of us sleep alone, so make sure you become good friends with your Self.

Before you get out there, you need to find a time to get real.

'Abundance comes from within.
It comes through thought, intention, attention,
and expectation.'
~ Deepak Chopra

Story 11.

"What you focus on, expands in your life," he recalled the mantra that the author referred to. It was during one of those extremely humid evenings in the Gulf, and the boy was, yet again, on the phone with his friend. There was barely anything to do in his spare time, at least out of the choices the boy preferred, which made him use most of his after-work freedom to work out, read, write, call his loved ones, and watch movies. He liked to explore the area, and so he did from time to time, but the city itself wasn't too big either, and by the time the fourth month of his deployment/employment rolled in, he was familiar with most of it. *"What he refers to is the fact that we choose what we put our attention on, and that inevitably becomes bigger,"* he continued, *"at least in our mind's eye."* He liked these evening conversations with his friends, especially the few that were happy to discuss difficult, often challenging to grasp or face, topics. He believed that such discussions were making them better as people and offered a great number of benefits in terms of life-preparedness.

"But how about a poor person, let's say," his friend asked, *"how are they supposed to focus their attention on not being poor if that's all they are able to see and experience?"* *"I think that's a great example,"* the boy parried instantaneously, *"according to his teachings, they still have the choice on what to focus on."* *"They can see what they lack or see what they can do to change their situation,"* he connected the mental dots within his mind, *"it's not like you can think of being poor and successfully consider the ways of making money at the same time."*

He continued his walk down the main road, heading towards the park, where he often took shelter in the evenings to breathe, relax, call a friend, or jog under the stars. His stride was brisk but relaxed, as he crossed the street and turned the corner in front of the park's gate. There were a few people around, some with their children. He thought of the many challenges, still far beyond his imagination, that bringing up a kid has to offer. He pondered this as he crossed the gate's line and continued down the wide path surrounded by the bushes and trees of the local flora.

"I guess it's like with anything really," his friend finally responded, "what you hold in the mind or care about is likely to be noticed quicker than other things and situations." "Exactly," the boy smiled at the passer-by, "a good example is your family car." "I could bet you a tenner that whenever you see the same model of a car on the street, your reaction to it is stronger than if it was any other model," he added, "like literally, most of the cars we do not even pay attention to, but those few we know, we will see anytime, anywhere."

They chuckled. It was obvious that such an ordinary example was easy to comprehend and discuss, but the boy did feel a little concerned about the intricacies of a more elaborate and potentially sensitive topic. "Can this be applied to anything we encounter in life though?" he asked somewhat rhetorically. The two thought about it for quite some time. One was driving his car back from work, while the other was already nearing the middle of the park. "I think it can," his colleague said after a moment, "think about it, why wouldn't it?"

"Only because we may find it more challenging, that doesn't mean it is not possible," he continued, "and if we do assume that the writer was right and it feels to me like he actually did, then picking and choosing to which aspect of our life this, let's say rule, applies is a fragile assumption." "If we could be choosing what to apply this attention-choosing dynamic, wouldn't we be already participating in it anyhow?" he added with confusion, "that's some mind-bender for you!" This time they heartily laughed. "I guess you're right," the boy answered, noticing yet another family with children walking across the path, "for any universal rule we choose to accept, we have to accept it universally and abandon any need of choosing where this rule would apply."

"Gravity works anywhere in the Universe, that we know of," his friend added, "it's not like we can choose to leave it not working in our backyard."

Chapter 11. Where Attention Goes

At this point, we should consider the witty quote from Deepak Chopra's "Seven Spiritual Laws of Success". I wholeheartedly recommend this book to anyone interested in exploring the 'alchemy' behind success from a more spiritual standpoint. Maybe this is something you'd like to explore. If so, please follow the link in the notes and get yourself a copy. Anyway, I want to share with you this beautiful phrase, which helped me many times, especially when the going got too hard to handle, or when I didn't know exactly where to focus my efforts. "Attention energizes, intention transforms,"[2] claims the author. As these are two tightly interlinked ideas, we shall dissect them one next to the other, and see how their wisdom could help us deal with our own life drama. It's quite simple, really! I bet you already have some idea of what I am about to state, but let's hold our horses and take it one word at a time...

You might remember from our body scan exercise earlier in the book that whenever you place your attention's gaze on one area, other spaces become a little blurry. It's a lot like looking through a magnifying glass. Whatever you aim at becomes sharper and more visible, whereas the area surrounding your object of observation dissolves into blurriness. The very same mechanism affects our interaction with the world around us and with our emotions on the daily basis. Whatever you may place your attention on will gain in intensity and offer a sharper image of itself to you. Like through the magnifying glass, you make this activity, thing, emotion, or idea bigger in your mind's eye. It does not necessarily inflate the

---

[2] *The Seven Spiritual Laws of Success* by Deepak Chopra

actual item, but it makes it more prominent from your perspective. This is what 'attention energizing' is all about. Your attention, as powerful as it is, can empower or diminish the importance of a thing, person, event, emotion, or idea in your perception's field. And the interesting part is, that you're using this ability all the time, even if you do it subconsciously. "Whatever you focus on, expands in your life." If you train daily and have a plan to run a marathon, the marathon's idea slowly but surely gains in intensity, probability, and power. Like feeding an animal or watering a plant, you are providing your goal with more and more sustenance, which will allow you to achieve it. You give it your attention, and so it gains in importance and grows. It is the same with our emotional states, perspectives on what has happened or what may happen, and everything else. The good thing about this is that we can learn to be more aware of these choices and choose these 'priorities of attention' more skilfully. The challenge lies, however, in putting it into practice and 'untying' the subconscious patterns of behaviour (both thought and physical ones), which we've grown to treat as our natural states up to this day. Each of us carries plenty of these subconscious programs within. We learn them from our parents, peers, and personal experiences. We also actively pick up new such attitudes and modes of being from those we spend the most time with, which is why becoming aware of yourself, and your surroundings is a great and the only way of stopping this cycle of letting other's influence affect our joy, happiness, and attitude. "Attention energizes", so make sure you pay attention to what your attention wants to pay its due, and recognize the things, people, ideas, and emotional states you'd like to primarily focus on.

What you focus on, expands in your life, so make the best choice for yourself and your well-being, and repeat this 'picking practice' each day, until it becomes your second nature. That's the trick! To make it into an automated activity, rather than an energy-demanding inner struggle. Before we jump into the second part of the quote, I want to offer you a simple practice tool, which can greatly expand your ability to put attention on the more positive aspects of your life. Gratitude practice is truly a life-changing solution. It doesn't need to be complex or overly time-consuming. It can be as small as writing down five to ten things you are grateful for in the evening or in the morning. These can include anything from the day's weather to a loved one's health, etc. Just write down in present tense what you are grateful for. You can use the classic structure of 'I am so happy and grateful now that...'. As easy as that! I have been using this technique for more than three years now, and truly it has done wonders for me. Like a sweet treat on a sad day or a warm, cosy blanket on a winter morning, this practice can help you shift your naturally problem-solving, problem-focused mind to notice the beauty, blessings, and good aspects of your life. And I am certain, whatever you may be going through, you have many of them to be grateful for. Give it a try! I am so happy and grateful now that...

[WRITE HERE]

Okay, the second part of Deepak's phrase claims that 'intention transforms'. This one may be a little bit trickier to explain, as we will not relate to much of a 'physical transformation', which you may be more familiar with. This part is all about 'changing the situation, outcome, or attitude'. It's about 'transforming your world'. My favorite example to use is the one of dating. Love, after all, speaks to us all, and I expect you have plenty to say on the matter as well. Everyone does. When it comes to attraction and love, we can relate this image of 'intention transforming' something to a case of two people. Let's say, they have bumped into one another on the staircase. Let's take the perspective of one of them and make it our own, by assuming that they secretly adore the other one. They want to date them and be together, but they are yet to 'make a move'. In this case, the intention of 'dating the other' becomes the driving force for what is yet to happen. Our hero may invite the other person out or they may crack a joke, hoping to initiate a conversation, which could lead to them grabbing a coffee after work. Whatever the case may be, their intention dictates the direction, in which this relationship may go. It is important to note, at this point, that nothing is certain, and everything is relative, so do not expect that just by 'placing intention' you are already acquiring, achieving, or becoming what you intend for. There will always be the other person's perspective and intention, the randomness factor the Universe is filled with, and the many parallel influences, that may steer your intention's ship towards one shore or another. In other words, it's not all up to you! You may want to drop down on the floor and start kicking your legs and punching the air presenting the defiance against these 'out of your control' pieces of the puzzle, but I would advise you to do otherwise. There is nothing you can do about the things you cannot do anything about. It's just how it is. If everything was completely up to you, life would be rather bland and far from interesting. Without chaos, there couldn't be any order, so instead of mulling over the unfairness of this world, focus on what is in your power. And may I remind you, there is plenty of that!

Your intention can and constantly does participate in creating your world. It may not take the grey, nasty building opposite your window down, but it could help you in covering it with ivy, and making it look nicer. You can intend on doing something and, as long as you're committed to making it happen, the chances of success are in your favor. A good example of this power in action is the production of anything (a film, a painting, an invention), which always must emerge from the initial idea mixed with the intention of the creator to actually 'make it happen'. And so, it can work for you! To summarize, 'attention energizes' by allowing your physical and mental capacity to pull whatever you attend to towards the desired outcome, whereas 'intention transforms' by helping you influence the outcome, create something new, or change the dynamic, which participates in your life. Whatever you may wish to attend to and intend for, it is yours to take, become, experience, or attract. You have to give it your all and keep your head up. From my experience, whatever we wish for happens in one way or another, so 'be careful what you wish for', and do not hesitate to act when the wishing comes near…

Remember that 'energy flows where attention goes.'

'So then, by their fruits you will recognize them.'

~ Matthew 7:20

Story 12.

"Sharing your idea in seeking advice is completely different from sharing your plan in seeking praise," his mentor exclaimed, as they were discussing a challenging topic. "I'm not saying you should tell everyone about everything, but if you seek advice, make sure you specify what this advice should be referring to..." They were talking over the phone. The boy was walking down the seaside boulevard, while his friend and mentor was back in his office, one more meeting planned in his calendar. The time difference was big enough for one to finish his work, while the other was still about two hours in.

"Fair enough, but why wouldn't I then share the idea with my friends when I am only considering it?" he answered, "without much pressure, just to get to know their opinion..." "What use do you have of anyone's opinion?" his mentor sounded irritated, "isn't it the cheapest commodity in the world?" Silence. "Would you take a black bin bag from some stranger on the street, only because they said it's for free?" he added, "because that's what you are doing when you take advice from anyone, regardless of their expertise and ability to help you..." The boy thought about it for some time in silence. He did get the point. Speaking with people about one's plans, when their ability to advise is extremely low, does pose some unnecessary risks and potential confusion. "Moreover," his teacher continued, "if you talk with others about something they do not see as appropriate or smart to do, you are likely going to hear about all the reasons why you shouldn't do it in the first place!" "It can be disheartening," the boy admitted. "Disheartening," his mentor

almost laughed, "for an idea in its early stage, it is almost always deadly!"

Their conversation continued for some time, as the teacher explained the many forms of dialogue, which people often took advantage of to gain praise from others. He mentioned how dangerous such interaction can be to any project or an idea, as the motivation behind the activity lessens with each time someone's approval is gained. "As if they have already made it, people feel better because of others' appraisal, even though they have not even started," he said, "and then they never do..." "You should first understand your intentions, and then decide whether to speak or not..." The sentence rang in the boy's ears as he was walking across the sandy part of the boulevard. "If you need the ego boost, fair enough, talk about your plans all you want," his mentor continued, "but if you're smarter than that and what you need is appropriate advice, do not talk about your plans and ideas with anyone who isn't suitable to advise you..." "In other words, only ask the opinion of those who succeeded in the kind of things you are trying to do and who wish you well," he added.

After disconnecting, the boy walked slowly back to his flat, thinking of these pieces of wisdom his teacher offered him. He did understand the benefit of keeping the plans to himself, especially at their earliest stage, but he felt slightly annoyed at the idea that his own friends would discourage his ideas. "I do not believe that's true," he concluded, "at least not the ones that I call my best friends..." "Maybe you are right," he heard a thought formulated within, as if his mentor was still there, "but what if they would do so out of care for you, rather than malicious motives?" "I guess *that could happen," he admitted, "in the end, we often worry about others when what they are doing seems impossible or dangerous to us…" "I guess he might be right in the end…"*

Chapter 12. Keep Your Plans to Yourself

Since we've already touched on the idea of intentional activity and attention's power, it's about time I introduce you to one of the most important parts of any striving or choice-making whatsoever. This is where, intuitively, you may find yourself in complete disagreement, and for a good reason. As serious about our goals and wishes as we may be, keeping them to ourselves does not necessarily feel intuitive. Often, we want to share the hopeful news with the world. Sometimes to gain acceptance and encouragement, sometimes to boast and seek praise, and sometimes simply to tell our conversation partner where we are heading for the sake of saying something interesting. Of course, this is not to say you should completely withdraw from expressing any of your perspectives and plans to anyone. That is not the case. There is, however, as we will discuss, a certain metric you should use, whenever deciding with whom to share your ideas and dreams and when...

Before we talk about others, let's focus on ourselves. After all, by changing our own behavioural patterns, we can affect our lives much more than by trying to make any changes in anyone around us. "Live and let live," remember? Let others be as they are and do your homework first. As Jordan Peterson invites us in his great book "12 Rules for Life" – 'set your house in perfect order before you criticize the world[3]. Clean up your own mess before you tell others to clean theirs.

When it comes to our inner world, keeping plans and ideas to ourselves can do us plenty of good. There are three reasons why this is true, and whichever of these you may find the most suited to your character and circumstance, I would invite you to ponder it and really reflect on how you acted out these tendencies in the past. Allow your past experience to inform you and help your present, but do not be too hard on yourself. What's done is done. Get over it and thrive.

Firstly, most of us, most people in general, are driven by ego. It is nothing inherently bad, as it is a part of our nature, but over the course of the past few centuries, we have grown less and less conscious of this aptitude, which made all things slightly messier than they would be otherwise. To recognize whether ego is behind the steering wheel of your life, investigate the experiences that confronted you with your weakness of some kind. Do you usually find excuses for your shortcomings and lack of action? Do you often mention your great plans and upcoming events to others in a way that invites their praise and approval? Do you like to be at the center of attention in a conversation, even if its topic is far from what would place you in its most prominent space? In other words, do you feel like you need to explain and reason your place wherever you are? These kinds of attitudes may seem negative, but let's not be too hard on ourselves. They are simply human. They are a part of our nature and until recognized and acted upon, they

---

[3] *12 Rules for Life: An Antidote to Chaos* by Jordan B. Peterson

will play a role in our life's activity. It's just how we work sometimes. Not necessarily proud, but certainly egodriven. In this case, keeping your plan-sharing and ideas-explaining to yourself can help you keep your ego in check and develop a more friendly, easy-going attitude when speaking with others. Your confidence does not rely on what you will be doing in the future since 'the future never comes'. There is only here and now, so you might as well focus on developing more self-confidence based on 'who you are', not 'who you may become'.

It may sound complex, but it really isn't. A quick recap of your previous successes will help you recognize the inner strength you possess and remind you that there is no reason for your ego to grow from the illusion of the future. What you plan isn't what you do until it's done, so maybe keep it to yourself, check your ego, and simply become more of who you are right here, right now. The second side-effect of premature boasting or plan-sharing can seriously hinder the plausibility of that hoped-for result ever actualizing. I know, it may sound counterintuitive, but whenever you share your plans and gain recognition of them from others, you are already experiencing a boost of dopamine – the achievement-driving hormone which flushes your brain with pleasant sensations. Dopamine is a very useful hormone, which can seriously improve your well-being and life satisfaction, but since it is released whenever any kind of achievement, both illusory and real (including those addiction-driven ones) takes place, you can easily mess yourself up by letting it abuse you. It is important to note that the same hormone is released when one takes drugs, wins a competition, eats food, receives a notification on the smartphone, or smokes a cigarette. You may already see why it can be a disservice to your future self to allow dopamine-driven activities to take the lead. By gaining the satisfaction of experiencing your plan already done, even though you may not have even taken the first step towards it, you are lessening the actual motivation to pursue that goal. Of course, this may not diminish your will and intent enough to completely stop, but it is said to slow down, if not stall the process, since the illusory payoff inside the brain can easily trick you into believing the actual payoff isn't that important. You said you're going to do something, you got patted on the back for your initiative, you felt the 'dopamine rush', and you subconsciously realized it is no longer important to pursue that goal. Why would you? After all, you've already achieved its results, right? This trap of 'telling others about your plans' is especially dangerous because it does not imply the ego's control and does not need the applause of the whole room. The dopamine release can happen with acknowledgment as small as a smile or a nod from your loved one. They are happy for you to be taking the step and they show it. You get the hit, you feel satisfied, and the plan goes back to the wardrobe. If this kind of situation sounds familiar, get into the habit of keeping your plans to yourself until you have AT LEAST made some progress towards making them a reality. It is much harder to stop a rolling vehicle than one that is just about to start the drive.

The third aspect of 'keeping it to yourself' regarding your approach deals with the risk, which is certainly a part of everyone's life from time to time. We all have to live with others, and we all are different in so many ways it is hard to imagine. Whereas this third point is somewhat connected to people around you, it is nevertheless your own to tackle internally and not to be taken lightly. No one else can help you avoid this aspect of over-exposing your goals and ideas better than yourself. It is up to you, and you will have to do the work if you want to avoid the effects of this miscalculation. People have different opinions. Everyone has plenty of them, and most of us are more than happy to share them with the world whenever the opportunity arises. While it is not necessarily useful to go around the room telling everyone what you think is best, we all do that at some point and most likely won't stop anytime soon. This is due to the fact that, even when we genuinely want to help, we can only refer to our own knowledge, experience, and insight, providing a highly personalized, often faulty opinion. It is for this reason why, under no circumstances, should you share your plans and ideas with others unless you WANT to hear their opinion about it. They will have no other choice but to let you know their thoughts if you invite them to do so, because that is the only thing they know. Of course, you may find the few unique individuals whose self-understanding arrived at such depths that they no longer react to others by explaining and projecting their own perspectives at anyone, but these individuals are rare and often only manage such a level of self-restraint after many years of mindful practice. For the majority of us, sharing the things we know is the only way of participating in the conversation, and therefore, whenever you decide to explain your plan or idea to another, expect them to respond with their opinion. This may not sound too bad if you are dead set and completely confident about your plan, but if there is the tiniest speck of doubt within you, and you unluckily shared your goal with a person who does not see it as something possible (maybe because they failed in a similar circumstance before), you are risking your own confidence and success. They may manage to put out your soul's fire with their friendly opinion, which they will share with the best of their intentions. Without planning it, they may completely disarm your plan, which is why you should think twice before you share anything of such a future-based quality with another. And if you do, remind yourself that their previous experience has little to do with your future, and should be taken with a hefty pinch of salt. You will have to stick to your guns, so you better be prepared for it if you do…

In terms of the other side, I believe we should talk about only one reason, which is all-encompassing in its quality to make or break anyone's spirit. I will briefly mention a more abstract part of this warning, but please feel free to dismiss it if you do not consider the spiritual, the energetic or unseen, as something worth thinking about. You have all the right to do so, and so I shall leave it for you to ponder and decide. Whenever you share your plans with another, you open your heart's mind for them to see. The question I want you to consider is: what do they wish for you? Some people, even the closest to us, can actually go against the plans, ideas, and aspirations we may hold dear. Sometimes they do so out of concern for our well-being, sometimes they may do so out of jealousy, which arises when their ego notices someone else succeeding in the area they failed in, sometimes it is because they simply wish you badly. It is difficult to say, which of these is most destructive, as all of them can easily impact your likelihood of success and satisfaction. As we have previously mentioned, whenever you share your plans, you risk hearing what others have to say on the matter, and those comments may not necessarily be the most positive and encouraging ones. Sometimes they are, sometimes they are not. This challenge and potential obstacle grow even bigger if the person you share your vision with does not actually wish to see you succeed. If, for whatever reason, they would rather see you stay the way you are and not achieve the success you strive for, you have unconsciously added another obstacle to your journey.

This may sound bad and disheartening, and I truly wish you do not encounter anyone in your life with such an attitude towards you. However, considering the complexity of the world and the many different circumstances that facilitate our lives, it is hard to believe you will be so uniquely lucky as to avoid it throughout your whole life journey. That is why, instead of 'turning your gaze away' and pretending this issue does not exist in your life, recognize it for what it is and simply pay more attention to who you share your plans and dreams with. Becoming more aware of yourself will greatly increase your ability to become aware of those around you. So, as we continue with this book, you shall be on the right path, my friend…

To summarize, then, by keeping plans, especially in their early stages, to yourself, you can avoid creating more openings for your wish to be punctured and blown away. You strengthen your self-confidence by first taking steps towards achievement instead of boasting before anything happens, and you keep your ego in check if you decide to "show with your actions, not your words". Also, by keeping your desires within your mind and the trusted circle of your closest allies, you avoid the risk of allowing someone whose intentions towards you may not be too pure to sabotage your success. And the last thing that I promised to mention in this chapter, in terms of sharing your plans with others, is this: if you believe that there is a certain level of energy in the world, which is yet to be determined—some scriptures call it life energy, some people refer to it as ether, some simply call it intentional thinking—then you should bear in mind this simple rule: the more people wish you well, the more powerful your plan for success is; the more people wish you unwell, the more powerful the obstacles on your journey may be. So, if you wish to take my advice to heart, I will invite you to first do and then say what you did, because this way, you are minimizing the likelihood of anyone and anything stopping you from attaining your goal…

Let your actions speak for you and keep your plans to yourself.

'Most people in the world
don't really use their brains to think.
And people who don't think are the ones
who don't listen to others.'
~ Haruki Murakami in 1Q84

Story 13

The seaside breeze felt pleasant on her face. The time of lesser hotness and longer walks in the sun without the risk of sunstroke was coming around. The girl was happy about it. She felt as if it had been years since the last time, she could go outside for more than an hour without worrying about her face's skin or overheating her head. "Side effects of living in the Middle East," she murmured light-heartedly. Most of her friends did not understand the choices she made, especially the one about leaving her hometown for a job assignment in the middle of the desert. She also thought about it from time to time. Not because she worried about the rightness of the choice, but rather the circumstances and decisions that led to her coming here. She walked past an ice cream stand, making sure she didn't look in its direction. "No time for ice cream," she said to herself quietly, "I've got to eat cleaner..." Thinking of this, she approached a stone wall, which stood between the two sides of the parking lot by the beach. Her shirt waved in the wind as she sat on top of the wall and closed her eyes. She had been planning to meditate for quite some time already but didn't know which place to choose. After walking for a quarter of an hour without making a choice, she realized that the best way to approach this decision was by simply executing the action on the next available wall or bench. "Keep it simple, stupid," she reminded herself of a phrase she once heard.

Sitting there, cross-legged, she took a few deep breaths and relaxed into the position that felt most appropriate for her body. Feeling into the rhythm of the breath, she knew there were quite a few things that her mind had to churn before a moment of quiet could be felt.

Her life's pace accelerated greatly since finishing university two years earlier. She travelled a fair bit, worked for multiple restaurants, event organizers, and agencies, when unexpectedly she encountered the opportunity to travel abroad with a job that promised to pay well and take care of the expenses. Of course, there was a price to it. Intensity. With back-to-back meetings and a great number of contacts to take care of, she felt overwhelmed from time to time, which her daily meditative practice was helping greatly. Trying to keep her mind in check, she would often have a momentary break to take a few breaths, refocus, and realign with how her body felt. It was a necessity, and it worked. Sitting there, she listened to the sounds of the world around her before, yet another strain of thoughts would pinch her easily distracted mind. She could hear the subtle hum of the sea against the shore, the windy waves making her hair dance freely around her face, the city's rhythm filled with cars, barely audible voices, and sporadic blares of anger expressed with the use of the car's very own horn. She allowed her attention to rest in that space for some time before her thinking would step in for another round. Familiar with the process, she accepted its difficulty. "Never fully free of thoughts," she thought, "the path is the goal," she added.

Recognizing the qualities that her participation in the quiet dance of the world consisted of, she took the deepest breath thus far and opened her eyes peacefully. The world shined with colour and light, as the glare of the sea offered an enhanced palette of shades to participate in this visual experience of hers. She looked down the path thinking of the ice cream salesperson, whose work seemed to her a greater burden than any of the days at the office could be. She wondered if they were stuck there without a choice or rather passionate about the ice cream so much, they had long decided to dedicate their whole life to the practice of seaside-path-ice-cream-sales-in-the-scorching-sun. She smiled at the thought. "Seaside-path ice cream professional," she recited what the mind had written across the screen of her inner world, "funny..." She got up from the wall and walked towards the ice cream stand. She decided against buying the treat but wanted to have a chat with the salesman. She wondered whether they would understand one another. She wondered what made him choose this line of work. Or maybe it wasn't a choice... Anticipating the potential outcomes, she noticed the waves of thoughts that splashed against the shore of her mind as she approached him. "Let go and listen," she commanded herself, "whatever you may think is wrong unless you give him a chance to tell you his story..."

Chapter 13. Listen Closely

There is no doubt that whenever we are truly listened to by another, we feel appreciated and deeply recognized. To be heard, truly heard, is one of the most beautiful experiences one can find themselves in. I am certain that you've also had these moments before when your loved one, your parent, or your friend gave you the kind of attention that completely disappeared the world around you both. It sometimes makes me feel as if the world has dissolved around me; like there is no one else but us two, entangled in the conversation. Being heard is a great gift to both give and receive... But I don't want to only talk about listening to others in this short but sweet chapter. I want to discuss with you the three types of listening: listening to others, listening to the world around you, and, most importantly, listening to yourself. As we have already touched a little on each of these areas, we will simply build upon the previous thoughts and 'connect the dots' to piece it all together and make sense of what the world may expect of us to hear.

Firstly, as we've already stated, listening to others is a great way of connecting with and giving appreciation to those around you. By giving them undivided attention, you offer people the space in which they can truly express whatever is on their mind's heart. Like the spotlight of attention, we've explored in the meditative part of our journey, this experience of attentive silence pointed at the other gives them the chance to feel like a star on stage. It is their time to shine. Their time to let you know about their world. How exciting is that...?! Of course, this kind of attitude of attention pays off regardless of how deep of a relation you might have with the person in question. Both in social life and business, offering such a space to your partner in conversation is a great way of fostering a culture of respect and connection. You also gain the ultimate opportunity to see into the other person's mind or heart, which can help you negotiate a better deal for you both, resolve troubles that may have arisen from poor communication, or simply recognize their beautiful, unique ways of being and give them the due praise. It is the kind of appreciation that builds bridges stronger than anything else. It is also something we, in our day and age, chronically lack, as the world is rapidly becoming more technologically connected and socially divided with each new addition and invention in the 'social media' sphere. It is quite a paradox that something called 'social media' managed to diminish people's ability to socialize, and created unnecessary walls between strangers, leaving most of us unfulfilled, lonely, and isolated. It is about time we leave the phone on the side and have a real conversation. Only through mutual understanding and respect can we build a connection that will lead to a more friendly and welcoming world.

The second way of listening to life's parts is all about listening to your surroundings. A good way to practice this ability is to simply contemplate nature. You could take a calm stroll in the park, visit a secluded part of the beach, walk through the forest on your own or with a friend (but while staying quiet), or simply sit down under a tree with your eyes closed. The trick to empowering this internal-to-external synchronization is to leave all distractions behind or at least turn them off. Without music, apps, discussions about news, and anything else that keeps your attention within the logical part of your mind, your body and the more intuitive part of the brain will be able to come on stage. Becoming more aware of the world around you, exactly where you are, exactly how you are in that space, is a powerful shortcut towards more calm and flowing living. Your peace and calm depend on your ways of being, and if you do not give yourself the space to simply be without the distractions of the world, which scream and beg for your attention, you won't feel completely at ease and in touch with the nature of your existence. In other words, you may come to understand yourself better and recognize your place in this world if you allow the world to be with you uninterrupted. Like the attention given to your friend, you should give attention to Mother Nature and see what she has to say.

The third piece of this listening puzzle is all about listening to your inner self. Becoming one with your 'gut,' your 'intuition,' your 'soul'—you can call it whatever you want. You may wish to leave it unnamed as well. It doesn't really matter, as long as you acknowledge it as a part of you and let it play a more significant role in your daily life. Give it the love it deserves and see it come out of its shyness-filled room. To foster this kind of self-love, you can use a few simple techniques of mindful living. You may want to start by practicing meditation, which is nothing more than sitting without much purpose and becoming aware of one's own awareness. Making it simple is the key—just focus on your breathing. Nothing more. This kind of practice can help you recognize what you may want to pay more attention to while you go about your daily activities throughout your week. I would suggest starting with this kind of intentional sitting because practicing this kind of awareness of awareness while actively participating in daily life can be too much to handle for a beginner like me and you. There are many great sources of insight you may want to explore while learning more about mindfulness and meditative techniques, but one thing you can start to apply today is this: simply schedule a time in your day when you calm your mind and observe yourself. Do this daily, and you'll see improvements in your focus and self-care levels in no time. Sometimes, people feel uneasy with being so passive in their meditation, which is why many great people throughout the ages invited the public to practice mindfulness while doing repetitive and rather mindless jobs, such as dishwashing, cleaning, running, working out, etc. You may want to try some of these activities if you feel like calm sitting down is not for you.

At this point, I shall mention again the powerful tool of 'morning pages' writing[4], which I have been practicing daily in the morning, mentioned in Julia Cameron's "The Artist's Way" book. This written meditation is a great option for anyone who feels like they appreciate writing and do not feel patient or calm enough to be sitting down to meditate. The technique invites you to simply write out three A4 pages of your 'stream of thoughts.' No rules. No expectations. No bad answers. You just write anything and everything that your mind invites you to consider. This is one of the best ways to put the thoughts out of your mind, see them on paper, and observe what dwells in your mind on a daily basis. It can also be used as a kind of journal, which is an additional plus! As you can see, there are quite a few ways of listening in life. You can listen to others, the world, and yourself. You should, to be honest, listen to all these quite deeply; especially to yourself. Through listening more and speaking less, you will gain a greater understanding of everything that happens in your life, and this, in

---

[4] *The Artist's Way* by Julia Cameron

turn, will inevitably improve your well-being while enhancing the way people interact with you. If you pay great attention to the world, many wonders will become apparent. It only takes some practice and intention.

So, keep calm and listen closely…

'Truth never damages a cause that is just.'
～ Mahatma Gandhi

Story 14.

"If there is one truth, about which everyone should care, it is most likely impossible for us to see it and agree upon it, which means, in fact, that no matter whether it is or it isn't, we should primarily focus on our own truth..." The statement expressed by the speaker has put both the daughter and her mom in a state of doubt. *"So, nothing is inherently real,"* the girl started. *"I told you, it's all an illusion and nothing matters, just like my favorite singer claims,"* she announced triumphantly, looking at her parent. They were inside the shopping mall on their way to the cinema when, upon encountering a crowd of bystanders paying attention to something or someone, they moved closer to the source of the commotion and found this man simply speaking. He was wearing what looked like a striking hybrid of a priest's robe and a party suit, his shoulders covered in sparkly glitter, and a hat, which reminded the girl of the pirate movie she was so fond of. He was standing on top of a suitcase and, as it appeared, preached. *"What you can see here, you, the bystanders who decided to grant me some of your attention and hopefully a dime,"* he paused to allow the few laughs and chuckles to pass, *"is not exactly, or at least not in its fullness, what actually is taking place." "Supposedly, I am standing on this box, and, if I am not mistaken, there are quite a few people staring at me with plenty of scepticism, as I speak these words..."* Another wave of chuckles followed. *"...but in terms of what the perception of the reality of each of us is being experienced right this moment, only us, one by one, can actually tell and attempt to describe it..." "In other words, we are not seeing, hearing, and experiencing the same thing!"* he exclaimed and looked around at the gazing crowd. The girl frowned, as her pondering abilities were being challenged.

She thought of the idea which the weird-looking man was describing. "Each of us sees it differently," he continued, "and of course, we have agreed, thanks to our language, on a certain array of concepts, words, and ideas, but ultimately, at its very core, we are all experiencing only..." He took a pause to allow the word to resonate in the hearts and minds of his audience. "...only what we, in ourselves, are able to experience." "For what one considers madness, the other may find in their most valued dreams..." The speech ended and after a momentary pause, the man took off his hat and bowed to everyone. He said a few more words about his box, in which he was raising funds for something, and added loudly, "...so ask yourself, what kind of reality are you living in...?"

The two went to the cinema, enjoyed the movie, ate some popcorn, and found themselves walking back towards the mall's entrance, right where they encountered the crowd and the mysterious man a few hours earlier. "Do you think he is right?" the girl asked. Her mom was certainly thinking about this matter already, as she instantly looked at her daughter and answered with confidence, "I think that as much as he seemed a little weird, he has got a point..." "We don't see eye to eye," she added, "that's true." The girl thought about these ideas, as she went about her evening activities and chores. It was Sunday, so with school starting the next day, she had some things to finish before the weekend would end. Sitting at her desk, she opened her diary and wrote down a few sentences about the day she had spent with her mom. They went for a nice lunch, bought some great books at the store, and went to the cinema. And then there was the speaking man. The glittery priest. "Weird man talking about differences of perspective," she wrote down without much thought. Looking at the sentence, she pondered what her mother said earlier and asked herself what her perspective really was. "What does my reality look like...?"

Later that night, they were all sat together at the dinner table. Herself, her parents, and two brothers she shared her life with. Their dog was somewhere around the room as well, but the girl couldn't see it at the time. As they ate, she observed her family and thought about the different perspectives and thoughts each of them was experiencing at that moment. She was quite sure her younger brothers were only thinking about playing since they were no older than seven, but with her father and mother, she could not be so sure. Her father noticed the gaze and smiled, "What is this inquisitive look my dear?" The mother turned, already knowing the answer. "I was wondering what your truth is, Dad; what is your perspective," the girl answered with her mouth half full. "Perspective...? Truth...?" her father seemed surprised. "I wonder what that movie you watched today was about," he said, glancing at her mother. "But when it comes to my truth, it's all about my family..." "You are what I focus on the most these days," he added. The girl nodded, thinking to herself that she could have expected this answer. She continued her dinner without saying much as she pondered it all. Then, after taking the plates to the kitchen, she ran upstairs and sat down at her diary once more. "Thinking about your truth or your perspective is all about choosing what to think about," she wrote. "So, I should better figure out what I want to think about..."

Chapter 14. Speak Your Truth

"Have you noticed how many opinions there are in the world? I believe there are at least as many opinions as people, and considering each of us tends to have at least one point of view on each of the possible topics, one could say there is an endless number of opinions, with millions of new ones being generated as we speak. Although on their own, they are neither bad nor good, opinions can really cause us quite a bit of trouble if we allow them to influence us, rather than us influencing them. This applies both to third-person perspectives as well as our own. We either choose what we think and believe or get fed a mixture of thoughts and beliefs made by others. A great example of this phenomenon comes with the young age of being a child. Until you reach adolescence, you are likely to believe wholeheartedly in everything your parents say. They are, after all, your carers, people you trust fully and appreciate greatly. They are the ones who inspire your innermost beliefs and ideas about the world, yourself, and everything in between. To notice this dynamic, you can look back at your childhood and ask yourself a question: what do I believe based on that early time of my life?

For me, asking my father for advice and my mother for understanding was the basis of any important decision made in the early years of my life. Quite frankly, I have only recently stopped constantly going to my parents for help after I realized there are some topics I know more about than they do. That's the moment one must realize it's time to continue on their own, but also a moment to recognize and reflect on the lessons and beliefs we have received from these and many other people in our youth.

The issue with opinions, vocalized or only thought through, is the fact that they not only affect our mood at the time of being proposed but also inevitably influence our ways of being in the world once our mind (both subconscious and conscious) is exposed to them again and again if we have not been conditioned to dismiss their message. We are able to condition ourselves to see through the wrong views and leave them out on the sidewalk of our mind, but to do so, we first need to learn how to train our mind and change our beliefs. If everything does begin with a thought, then the best space to start should be within the frames of our thinking mind. So, let me ask you a question – what do you want to think about in your situation? Answering this type of question may not be too pleasant at first, as you will have to come to terms with the qualities your life consists of right now. If you are not where you want to be, you may want to stop reading here and now and go off to do some other thing, but I urge you to stay with it. It will not take long before you realize the ease with which you can improve your situation and thinking. When it comes to thinking about our experiences, ourselves, and the world, people are much more prone to notice the negative rather than the positive. According to Daniel Kahneman's 'Thinking, Fast and Slow,' we are about four times more likely to perceive the negative than the positive because we are wired to avoid and overcome challenges rather than enjoy the pleasures of success."[5]

This should help us understand why the majority of our thoughts are negative on a daily basis. Your mind, the ultimate machine in this world, is constantly on the lookout for danger, trouble, and

---

[5] *Thinking, Fast and Slow* by Daniel Kahneman

problems worth solving. That's where its attention will be pointed whenever a chance for a potential challenge appears. Instead of beating ourselves down for this quality, we should appreciate its ingenuity. We are, thanks to this nature of ours, the best problem-solvers in the known galaxy. We are the ultimate innovators. But, for the time being and for the needs of this chapter, let's just say it is not bad to think about the problems so much, as long as you give yourself the space to think about your successes and joyful moments as well. Let me elaborate on that…

As we've mentioned earlier, our thoughts (vocalized or internally heard) are the seeds of any reaction that takes place in our body and mind. We always try to act to our best ability and react to the things that happen around us. The thing is, our thoughts are, in their majority, based on the opinions and communications we have received from others and our surroundings. We pick up these statements, 'truths', and ideas and carry them in our minds, often mulling over their meaning and utility. If you drive down any street in your city today, you will likely encounter tens of advertisements and messages, which ask for your attention and invite you to take them along for the ride. Whether you like it or not, most of them will also jump into your mind's car anyway. They are prepared to hijack your attention because that's how they earn their dollar.

So, what can one do about all this? What can we do about the trouble of hearing too much useless nonsense all around us and constantly noticing negative, often self-loathing comments from within? First of all, we can become more mindful about them. By shining a light of recognition on their sorry-ass shadows, we can start the process of selection because once the message gets labelled as negative or useless, it becomes possible to let it go before its influence reaches our mind. Secondly, as you practice this 'thought-process observation', you can also decide what kind of thoughts you'd like to invite into your mind in their place. After all, you are the master of your mind, remember? Choose what kind of words, ideas, and inspiration you would like to hear on a daily basis and make sure to gift it to yourself. It can start with a simple 'I feel great today'. Repeating it daily will inevitably influence your mood, which in turn will influence the quality of your activity, which after some time will certainly influence your way of life.

As a third part, I would like you to become more conscious of what others are telling you and develop a more censorship-based attitude towards it all. Choose whom to listen to and who may be better left unheard. You need to guard the gates of your mind, so if some of your friends or acquaintances are too negative for you to simply dismiss their opinions, maybe it's best you part ways with them or at least decide to spend less time together, putting your health and sanity first.

Finally, similarly to the affirmations spoken daily, I believe you should get into a habit of 'gratitude listing'. This need not be anything big. As little as five gratitude sentences a day will do. Make sure, however, to do it consistently because our goal here isn't to only raise your mood once, as you read this little book, but to create a change that will improve your life in the long run.
Do these things every day and do not forget to 'speak your truth', which should consist of what you wish to think and what you act out on a daily basis, to make it into reality…

'Once you make a decision,
the universe conspires to make it happen.'
~ Ralph Waldo Emerson

Story 15.

"Go that way or the other," his friend exclaimed, "but whatever you do, get off that fence, bro!" They were sitting in the middle of the clearing, which was located in the centre of the forest near their houses. They grew up in this area. They knew it all too well and had spent countless days playing games, running around the neighbourhood, and meeting in the shade of the woods when the weather allowed. Now, the two were sitting on a trunk of a fallen tree and sipping their third or fourth can of beer (who would count the cans anyway?) as they quietly discussed the choices each of them had to make. One was considering dating the girl of his dreams, the other traveling the world without much of a plan. For either of them, their respective topics were rather important, not to say existential. After stubbing out a cigarette, one of the boys looked at the moon and repeated what he had said earlier, "You have to make a decision..." The other nodded, pondering his fate.

The forest was almost pitch-black by then. Their spontaneous meeting had happened late in the evening, and so by the time the fourth can was emptied, they were sitting in near-complete darkness. "Chaos," his friend added, "all is chaos, but what we make of it..." "I like that," he chuckled, "that's a good one, you should write about it... all is chaos, but what we make of it..." Their discussion involved recalling past experiences somewhat related to the discourse at hand, considering the timing of these potential actions and their likely impact on the lives of everyone affected by their choices, and many, many worries. One was unsure about making a move regarding his love for a woman, the other about making a move regarding a full-blown adventure travel, without much of a safety net. In each of their situations, there was barely anything to fall back on. Of course, there was also barely anything to lose since neither was yet doing or being with what or whom he wished for, but the necessary sacrifices each of the situations was to bring forth scared them a little. They discussed these concerns while enjoying each other's priceless company. "I guess not making a choice also counts as a way of choosing," one of the boys noted, "if by postponing your decision, you are stuck, isn't that a decision for the stuck-like state as a way out..." "It's easier said than done," countered the other, while both knew these ideas to be true. "But yeah, you are right, it is basically making a choice," he added promptly, ushered by his conscience, "because if you think about it, it basically means you are choosing not to do it while simply lying to yourself that 'you're still considering.'" He marked the inverted commas in the air and opened a fifth can. The fizzy sound punctured the natural silence of the forest. "Without a doubt, we have to make a decision as soon as possible," the other concluded, "whatever that decision may be..."

Upon bidding each other farewell and going their separate ways, as both lived on opposite sides of the forest from one another, they shook hands and thanked each other for a well-spent time. After a few steps in his direction, the boy caught a glimpse of a thought that followed the idea shared by his friend sometime earlier. He turned around, and seeing only darkness but knowing that his friend was still there and could hear him well, he exclaimed, "Let us go into the darkness of uncertainty with courage, because by making a choice we shine a light onto what's yet to come!" He heard an acclaiming scream of his friend and a loud wolf-like howl.

He howled as well. For better or for worse. Then they both laughed and went home.

Chapter 15. Decision Time

Like in any good book about the hero's journey into the unknown, we have to address the idea of decision-making on a deeper level. As we have already mentioned, a strong 'why' will propel you towards any kind of success and will keep you on your course when the going gets hard. The thing is, however, that as you continue your journey, while your 'why' may stay the same, your 'how' and 'what' will certainly shift and vary from one moment to another. You will have plenty of decisions to make each day. You already do. Reading this book is a decision. Brushing your teeth is a decision. Eating well or poorly is a decision. Every little activity, thing, and word you decide to bring into your life has its foundation in a decision. As James Clear beautifully stated, "Every action you take is a vote for the kind of person you wish to become."[6] It sometimes makes me dizzy to realize just how many decisions one must make on a daily basis to even survive, not to mention to thrive and succeed! Because of this, I need to warn you against becoming idle or slow in your decision-making. There can be no failure unless you quit, but there can be no progress unless you continue. And continuing will involve making a choice. In the same way, you choose which street to turn into as you are driving home from work, you have to decide on the paths you are going to take while becoming the best version of yourself and achieving your goals. These dilemmas will make or break you if you allow them to. On their own, they have no power over you, but the moment you start paying more attention to the doubts and potential hiccups down the road, you are already hitting the brakes. And you cannot hit the

---

[6] *Atomic Habits* by James Clear

brakes if you wish to get there anytime soon! Even less so if there are quite a few walls to break through as you go...

At this point, let me offer you a three-step strategy for making choices, which someone shared with me at some point in my life. It is not my original idea, but it is a helpful tool, and certainly, it can come in handy for people like me and you as we delve into the jungles of the unknown. The strategy involves considering your goal, the best-case scenario, and the worst-case scenario, whenever you have a decision to make. Let me explain...

Let's assume that you are about to choose a job. You have been applying for many and finally, as lucky and successful as you are, you got an offer from two of them. Both are somewhere on the spectrum of your interest, and both seem helpful in making progress on your journey. How do you choose the one...? The first step brings you back to the 'why' and the highest of your aspirations, which should be treated like a compass for your life's navigating techniques. What are you aiming for in the long run? What is your ultimate goal? For the purposes of explaining this strategy, consider the goal of becoming financially independent – being able to live off your passive income and not have to worry about money ever again. Now, let's apply this goal of ours to these two jobs and think about which one of them offers a better salary, more free time, greater learning opportunities, the potential for progress, and a healthier work environment. All of these aspects are important when choosing a job, but if you are concerned with making money quicker and retiring early, the last two are not as important as the first three. At this point, you prioritize which of these reasons for you to take the job are the most impactful on your highest goal attainment and continue onto steps two and three.

In the second stage, you have to assume the best-case scenario. What if everything happens exactly as you want, what will this job offer you? Where will you be after a year of working for this company? How will you feel after such time and experience? Where do you see this job taking you if everything goes swimmingly? Feel free to ponder this stage as much as you want but remember to make the decision within the decision timeframe, so do not leave it till later. Consider these things now, put them on paper for the best results, and really understand your best-case scenario with both of your options.

Finally, flip the script and think about the worst thing that could happen if you take either of these employments. Where will you end up in a year? What are your biggest doubts about the company? How will you feel and act after a year in such an organization? How much time, money, energy, or joy are you risking by choosing this employment? What's the worst that could happen? Writing these down may feel a little uneasy, but you will most likely recognize that the majority of the ideas written are just empty words. Depending on the severity of the decision you have to make, their impact may vary, but the idea stays the same. It is better to assume and understand the worst consequences to make a more informed decision, but it is as important to recognize that most of our potential-problem-thinking is just that – thinking. Do not shy away from writing these ideas down, as they will inevitably help your decision-making. Once you've done these three, you have probably already decided. For me, it often happens in the second stage. I get to write out or ponder the best-case scenarios and already feel the intuitive choice manifested within my body. Maybe it will be similar for you. Either way, you can leverage a good decision by putting these thoughts and ideas on paper. "An enemy you know is better than the enemy you don't know"... How true is that...?

To make a good decision, you will have to gain plenty of information about your options and ultimately choose as briskly as possible. It is often said that it is better to decide quickly and end up making a completely opposite decision a few days later than to sit 'on the fence' and look around for too long. One approach leads you to learn 'what you do not want' or maybe 'what is a bad decision', whereas the other keeps you in the mind-fuelled pursuit of theory, which seldom leads to any real progress. There are only a few very specific niches of the world's activity that demand more of this theory-based, cautious consideration over acting as a result of a considerate choice. Become the kind of person who decides promptly and acts courageously. Learn from your mistakes and shortcomings, and always assume both the best and the worst. These attitudes will help you shape your character to be 'all-weather' suited and 'crisis-proof'.

Ultimately, they will help you be prepared when the decision time comes.

'Good people are good,
because they've come to wisdom through failure.'
~ William Saroyan

Story 16.

"Isn't it funny that we suddenly want to learn so much, even though throughout school we barely paid attention?" she pointed out, as he sipped his chamomile tea. They were sitting in a café nearby her flat, and as their conversation reached the peak of educative focus, she decided to address this recently noticed phenomenon, "It's as if we have actually started our education, once Uni was over..." The boy agreed with her. Nodding softly, he took another sip before voicing any of his opinions on the matter. "It often happens like this with people who want more or something else from life than what is suggested, sort of prepared for them, by society..." They pondered his statement. "Quite frankly, you could find many geniuses and successful people who dropped out of Uni for this same reason," he added, "because they didn't see how it would help their passion or goal achievement..." The chuckle that followed was somewhat resembling the unfortunate realization of the debt taken up in haste, even before one knew why and what they would wish to place that debt on. "I do not regret going to University, however," the girl placed the book she was holding on the table, "it gave me so much in terms of social and 'adult life' skills, I can only be grateful for that." "Plus, it was plenty of fun, don't you think?" she added with a wide smile, while her mind recollected the many absurdities and pleasantries of the frivolous life on campus. "Yeah," he agreed, sinking into the soft cushion of these sweet memories, "it was a great experience for sure..."

Their conversation withdrew for some time. The girl got back to her reading, and the boy picked up his notebook and continued with the poem he was working on for the past two days. It was for his mother's birthday, and thinking of how to make it even better, he was definitely overthinking it a little. "It's okay to do that sometimes," he thought, "it's okay to overthink things that are too important for us not to do so..." The book the girl was reading dealt with the rules and tendencies within the realm of self-actualization and success. It was one of the many books her friend liked to read, and she actually borrowed it from him a week before. It was a good read with a few practical pointers. For the most part, however, it was a motivation of a sort, which somewhat frustrated her. She didn't need motivation, she needed guidance. Thinking of this, she reflected on the ways which the book suggested as the avenues for learning and developing one's skills. The mentioned few involved participating in a class activity, learning from written sources, internship at a chosen company, which necessitated the particular set of skills to be developed, or finding a mentor, who could guide the progress of their student. It was this last option that resonated with her the most. "I could definitely use some guidance and advisory from time to time," she noted. It was obvious that finding someone who knew where she should direct her efforts could speed up the process and alleviate some of the uncertainty-caused stress, which she tended to feel from time to time. As if he was reading her mind, her companion raised his chin and said, "It could be good to have a mentor, don't you think...?" Before she even had a chance to respond, he added, "I think I'll ask that guy I met through work if he could help me with taxes and all..." She simply nodded. Thinking if there was anyone in her life she could ask for such help, she looked back at the book and picked it up. The author was talking about the importance of learning, especially once the formal, contemporary education stage of one's life was over. They explained that oftentimes, the most important growth happens when people have to adapt out of necessity and when the learning process involves acting out whatever the interested is trying to practice. "Practice makes perfect," she thought, "practice makes progress," she added. They finished their drinks, paid the bill, and decided to take a stroll through the park before going back to their flats for more activities of the day. The boy was planning to go skating later, and she wanted to cook and do a little workout, before watching a movie with her flatmate. It was a nice weekend afternoon for both of them.

Walking down the main path of the park, she thought of the ways in which she could find guidance without having to impose herself on another person. "It takes a little bit of audacity and courage to ask for such support," she observed. The boy seemed to also be tackling some internal dialogue, as his forehead frowned into the green space of the summer afternoon. "Why don't we start a group to support one another in these things," he suddenly said, "like a brainstorming team or a mastermind-kind-of-a-group..." 'I like that idea', she smiled, 'sounds like a great way to teach one another!' And so, they did.

Chapter 16. In Pursuit of Wisdom

It often amazes me just how little credit is given to the knowledge and wisdom that a successful person may possess, when compared to the monetary wealth or worldly status they are admired for. Of course, it doesn't always have to be a straightforward dependency. Not every rich person is wise, and certainly not every wise person is rich, but there are a number of traits that can suggest the potential for success of each and every one of us, and wisdom is definitely a member of that category. You may be wondering why I would bring up the subject of gaining knowledge and becoming wise so late in the book. Shouldn't it be the first chapter, you may ask. Shouldn't it be the foundation, you may argue. Well, as much as I agree that it is a foundation, and a good one at that, I do not know if putting it any earlier in the book would make much difference, as ultimately my goal is to help you and myself by writing and reading these words. Nothing discourages one as much as being told what to do and just how behind they may already be by not having done it earlier, in the first place. In other words, would you be ready to hear about the importance of wisdom if I were to introduce it earlier? Yeah, I am not so sure about that either.

I think it's worth mentioning that becoming wise or at least knowledgeable in one's specialized niche is a process and a demanding one. It is not a five-day trick, a 10-minute fix, or a one-size-fits-all kind of solution. If it were, well... probably each of us would already be a genius by now. And I bet, as you look around, you can see that we are not. Far from that, to be honest. Acquiring knowledge, skill, and experience takes time and demands a certain level of self-discipline. Learning anything usually begins with turtle-like progress, which slowly accelerates, bending the learning curve more and more vertically. You may start small and initially struggle plenty. Quite frankly, I am sure you will. But then, at some point, there will come a time when suddenly these insights you've been gathering start to connect and make much more sense to you than ever before. They overwhelm the scale, and the centre of weight shifts. That, my dear, is 'the tipping point'. Inspired by Malcolm Gladwell's book The Tipping Point[7], I have decided to mention it here. Put simply, it is a moment when the accumulated number of whatever we are counting and analysing overwhelms the unaccumulated and tips the scale. You could call it a breakthrough. It's the moment when a brand becomes a worldwide sensation, the time when your online vlog suddenly, from one day to another, goes viral. It is the moment when, out of seeming nowhere, you get it all. You understand the why, how, when, and what about the subject you've been exploring. It's that 'AHA' moment that everyone talks about, but only a few get to experience.

So, as I mentioned, with learning anything new, you will have to first overcome the challenging era of knowing little and struggling to understand the most. Like going into a dark forest, until your eyes start to adapt to the overwhelming darkness, you have to survive the initial moment of pure, totally debilitating nothing-to-see-ness. And if the forest example does not resonate with your beautiful heart, consider how you feel when someone speaks a completely foreign language to you. It feels like a 'brain freeze' sometimes. It feels rather uncomfortable, a little frustrating, and

---

[7] *The Tipping Point: How Little Things Can Make A Big Difference* by Malcolm Gladwell

certainly impossible to make sense of. Well, the same is true for anything you want to explore and learn about. Initially, you will be a complete 'rookie', a person without any idea whatsoever about the nature of that which you've decided to learn about.

You must, however, remain resilient and weather out this difficult beginning if you want to learn and grow in the area of your interest. Once you've managed to understand the basics, the fun begins. The more you enjoy the learning process, the quicker you will acquire the knowledge you seek. So, I would urge you to choose the kind of things and ideas you feel deeply interested in exploring and start. Especially when it comes to our interests and out-of-work hobbies, the passion with which you approach them transforms their nature into something close to magical, if not pure magic. It's like with all the various subjects at school you had to do and those you actually enjoyed doing. I am sure there was a great difference between them in terms of your grades, your satisfaction level, and your attention span. And this is the best advice in terms of self-education one can give you – explore and learn about what interests you, and you will never want to stop exploring it. You will also make progress with the speed of light or even quicker.

The difficulty with pursuing wisdom, however, can be noted under the sign of 'all welcome', which may hang above your mind's door if you've decided to explore a certain subject. I would like you to refrain from hanging up such a sign anywhere else than outside your restaurant's, shop's, or house's door. Maybe it's best not to hang it anywhere and simply take everyone in when they come. Your choice, of course... Anyway, what I mean by this is the diligence with which you should always, and I mean always, consider the sources of the information you are 'taking in'. We live in a world saturated with information and misinformation. They intertwine, mix, and weaken each other's colours in the process. "Opinion is the cheapest commodity in the world," someone once said, and I wholeheartedly agree. Become a student of worthy sources and avoid acquiring and accepting knowledge, ideas, or opinions from anyone or anywhere that you are not sure of the intentions behind them.

As we mentioned earlier in the book, everyone has something to say about your stuff, and most of it won't be nice. The same is true for insight and information. There are hundreds of thousands of sources ready to 'educate' you. The question is, why would they want to do that? By understanding that not all knowledge is equal, you gain the freedom and independence to choose where and how to acquire the information you are seeking. You are in pursuit of wisdom, not in a magnetic-like situation about it. Do not let anyone or anything dictate your learning process unless you know their intentions and trust them fully. Your mind is your best and most precious tool, so you should sharpen it on high-quality stones, not side-road gravel.

A great way of determining whether someone or something should be 'listened to' as the source of acquired knowledge is to recognize the intention behind the given message. Is there a sale to be made based on you accepting their information? Will there be a likelihood of a certain emotion, which the new info causes you to feel? Would the person communicating this to you gain something with the successful convincing of yourself? What do they wish to see you do with that information when it is acquired?

Of course, often times it is rather challenging to register and determine these things straight away. Firstly, because the majority of the insight offered by others isn't actually theirs to give, and they just repeat an overheard babble from the previous interaction they've had. Secondly, the source of the potential knowledge may have a hidden agenda, unknown to the average bystander. Do not get me wrong; I do not want you to distrust everything and everyone, suddenly shutting yourself off from all the information available 'out there'. Not at all. By doing that, you would do yourself and your success a huge disfavour. Instead, I encourage you to simply be more mindful about the information and the sources of the information you encounter and take everything you hear with a pinch of proverbial salt. Take it in, digest on your own, ask the right questions, ponder the subject, and then draw a conclusion, which will determine whether the source and the insight is worth your time and attention.

You should become an expert censor of the information you are offered on a daily basis. You should 'stand guard at the door of your mind'[8]. Remember, we are bombarded with thousands of slogans, thoughts, ideas, product placements, and demands every day, and the majority of them are given to us out of a pure will for making money out of our attention and distraction. That is why I want you to 'become a guardian of your mind'. And a skilful one.

Although we will come back to the subject of mentorship and guidance later on, I believe it may be useful to touch on this topic here for just a moment. It can be especially useful to leverage our

---

[8] Quote from Jim Rohn

mindfulness practice and successful information filtering process with the support given by those we hold in high regard and trust. A mentor, similarly, to one's parent, can be a great ally in the fight against the overwhelm and misinformation offered by the media and the world these days. Depending on the subject and our partner's familiarity with the message's essence, we can ask our supporters about these things before we make the final decision on whether something or someone is worth listening to.

As we will elaborate on this later on, I just want you to realize that as long as someone is your role model and does hold the experience and knowledge necessary to address and discern the information's quality, you should reach out for their help whenever you feel it's needed. There is no more powerful support than that offered by someone who truly wishes us the best and is willing to help us on the journey we are undertaking.

To summarize, in pursuit of wisdom, you do have to keep your mind in check and your willpower strong. You should never assume the truthfulness of any new information without first at least pondering its essential meaning and the intention behind it. Sometimes you will find it easy to recognize why such information appears; sometimes, you will struggle to determine it. Regardless of this dynamic, you should do your diligent research and guard your mind from unnecessary, often intrusive communicates, which will leave you wanting, thinking, feeling, or being less mindful and in touch with your pursuit than before. As you dive deeper into the ocean of self-development and progress, you will swim with more and more dangerous sharks around, so get into a habit of polite distrust, taking everything with a little pinch of salt and only adopting the thought as your own, once they were truly reflected upon by yourself, potentially with the help of those you trust and aspire to emulate (for example, your mentors or parents). Moreover, do not ever stop learning about the things that make your heart dance, and if you are still hesitating whether to start on 'that adventure', this is your cue to do so…

Do so in pursuit of wisdom.

'I've failed over and over and over again in my life.
And that is why I succeed.'
~ Michael Jordan

Story 17.

"If you want to take the island, burn the boats," he recollected the statement from a centuries-old tale, "if you want to succeed in what you are doing, you need to give it your all..." It was the final round of the competition, and he was about to get into the ring. The hall was filled with teams from all over the UK, chanting their songs, encouraging, discouraging, and offending each of the fighters. Everyone had someone who cheered for them, and all had many who would rather see them fall. The finals were the real deal, and the boy knew it. No more anonymity, no more assistance from his colleagues, no more time to prepare, revise, and warm up endlessly. He got to that place for a reason, and it was time to make that reason come true.

"You will have to give it all you've got," his friend and fellow fighter said to him, as they were wrapping his hands with tape. "The other one knows how to kick, but you've got more power; use it." He knew he had no other choice. The other fighter was better with his leg kicks, that was true, but trusting the persistence factor beyond all else, the boy reprimanded any thoughts that seemed to anticipate failure.

"Until the bell rings," his friend screamed into his ear, just as the door into the main hall opened. "Do not stop even for a moment, until the bell rings..." They exchanged smiles; a few pats on the back added a little morale to the boy's spirit, and they went down the stairs toward the ring. The noise was unbearable. Sporadic shouts of his name, a few offensive comments, an invitation to die. All these voices became one tumultuous noise in his mind. He was

breathing deeply, trying to focus on nothing but the security and safety of his mind. He was completely engaged within.

The ropes were pulled away from one another, and the boy entered the ring. The lights were rather overwhelming to the eyes, which squinted involuntarily. He took another deep breath. "There is no way you can succeed if you do not completely give yourself up for what you're striving for," his mind recalled the speech he delivered to his team that same day, before they would all enter the center and start their fighting sprees. "It all depends on you."

"No one will do this for you," he said back then. "It is between you and you only, whether you decide with all you have to not give up until the end of the fight comes." "Remember that it is hesitation that stops dreams from coming true, hesitation and lack of action," he summarized. "Abandon these two, and you will be victorious..."

Thinking of this, he went into the middle of the ring, touched gloves, and fell into the abyss of adrenaline-fueled fight. He punched, dodged, kicked, moved, pivoted, smiled, groaned, and spat. He danced with the other fighter. He took punches and gave some. He tried his best. He did not stop. He did not hesitate. He left no stone unturned. And not without a fair deal of struggle, he won in the end.

"You won because of persistence, not technique or strength," his friend told him in the pub that same night. "You won because you wanted it more than that other guy..."

Chapter 17. No Matter What

As you may have already realized, the things we've been talking about are not so easy to put into practice when it comes to our daily lives. Oftentimes, we start something new because the excitement and the anticipation of success feel live and vivid, only to stop and abandon the project halfway through a few weeks or months later. It is so with health habits, career aspirations, New Year's resolutions, and almost anything one can wish to pick up and employ into their life "once and for all." I should probably start by asking your pardon, as I am not here to tell you that with the reading of this book, or any other book, for that matter, this "achievement" aimed process will become virtually different. You will have to do the work; you will have to tackle the challenges that arise, and you will have to make the necessary sacrifices to overcome the many ups and downs of your journey. I know, this isn't too motivating, but it is quite true. And, as I have already stated earlier, I'd much rather give you the truth and help you deal with it than offer you a snake-oil-like solution, which will only provide you with false hope at the start.

On the other hand, this certainty of hardship and promise of success by overcoming it can be exactly what you need to make progress and achieve your goals in the long run. With these things blatantly stated, out in the open for your eyes to see, you know what you're getting yourself into and knowing that, so many people have managed to pursue and attain their goals before you, you can find the necessary strength and belief to approach this challenge with all the power it requires. I am sure, since you are still with me, reading these words or listening to them via the audio version, you are one of those who do not quit easily if the payoff sounds attractive enough. And believe me, it is an attractive one. You know why…? Because it's yours. Completely personalized. An ideal end to the story you wish to tell. The thing is, for the story to end, it must first be told…

So, here we are, arriving at one of the most important aspects of any success in one's life. It applies to the spiritual, physical, mental, social, material, and any other sphere of our lives. It applies to everything that has been achieved and everything that is yet to come. It applies to you, me, the person outside your window, and the ancient human who lived on this planet so many centuries ago. It is considered to be the building block of fortune, achievement, satisfaction, strength, confidence, love, and anything in-between. It is the crème de la crème. The secret ingredient that makes the champions. And the irony of its secrecy is, it is fully available to all of us and has always been hiding in plain sight. Like anything worthy of our attention, it is invisible, indivisible, and completely, utterly special. It is the power that allows the drop of water to drill a hole in a rock-solid wall. It is the power of persistence, resolve, and perseverance. It is the power of the "no matter what" attitude.

We have already mentioned the impressive power which repetition and persistence can offer in terms of our goals. We've talked briefly about the way, in which by creating a strong belief, planning out the journey, choosing the right set of actions, and repeating them regularly, one can overcome many obstacles and allow the power of time and consistent effort determine the positive outcome of their struggle. The thing is, it is much easier said than done when it comes to making these steps and keeping the fire of our dreams lit.

That is why I would like to invite you for one more, maybe the most important, maybe the most counterintuitive, maybe the most challenging brainstorming session with me here today. Namely, we will have to figure out what drives our goals so much we would rather die than give up our efforts. Please be advised that if your wishes and dreams are not as important to you as to feel this way, you may need to review the previous chapters and find the kind of goals and achievements you would be willing to sacrifice your life for. It may sound a bit dramatic, I get that, but it is ultimately true. As Nietzsche once noted, "He who has a why can bear almost any how."[9] So, take a moment now, pick up your pen once more, and let's reflect on this.

Look at the list of goals you've created earlier. Look at what brings you joy, what you would be willing to do for free, and what you believe to be worth investing your life's time in. Because that's what this all is – an investment. You are a free person, able to choose what to do or not to do (of course, as long as you do not hurt anyone), so it is your responsibility to make the decision about the direction you're willing to move towards. The thing is, your choice should be in line with your dreams, ideas, and values, because if it isn't, the likelihood of you persisting when the going gets tough (which it will at times, believe me) is close to none. Consider all these dreams of yours and try to come up with a sentence or two for each of them. Why do you want to do, be, have,

---

[9] Quote from Friedrich Nietzsche

see, and experience these things? Why do they matter to you? Your answer may be something like, "I want to get in shape and stay healthy because by doing so, I will be able to enjoy my life to the fullest, will be of help to my family for longer, and will live a satisfying and long life." Simple and profound. Just the way we like it!

Go on then, take a few moments now and write at least one sentence for each of your major goals you've decided to pursue. The more powerful your why is, the stronger it will keep you in line, so recognize and choose the kind of words that bring up strong and deep emotions within you. The more serious this declaration of yours sounds, the more likely it is to stick.
[WRITE HERE]

Alright… You're done, aren't you…? Cool, let's continue.

Now, as you have these reasons written down, try to figure out if they all, or at least the majority of them, have something in common. Aren't they touching on the same emotional string if we were to dig deeper into each? For example, my wish to live healthily, to create meaningful work, and to see as much of the world as I can comes down to the essential quality I see in my life, which is the love of adventure. I want to be able both physically and mentally to enjoy, explore, and express as much of the awe I experience in the world as I can. I just adore the unique, absurd, often completely crazy qualities of this wonderful universe we happen to live in. So, look at your answers now and try to find the intentions, the motifs behind them. Is there anything that seems to appear in a few of them? A certain idea. A particular view. An emotional load that overwhelms your heart and mind when you feel it. Write these thoughts down and ponder them. Take some time. There is no rush.

We are almost there anyway, so let's savor these moments and make the most of them. I'll wait. Great, so you can hopefully see a certain overarching theme or a specific emotion that drives the reasons you've listed before. To make it even more powerful, we will now conduct a simple and quite interesting exercise I've picked up from one of the self-development courses a few years ago. I don't remember whose idea this is, so if it is yours (you, who are reading this), please forgive me. I deeply appreciate it, however, and want to share it with others as it was once shared with me. We will go into the essence of your 'why' by asking "Why is this important?" seven times. Each answer will be a cue for the next question to be asked. In this way, we will delve into the subconscious and often overlooked underlying motives of our activity. Bear with me, as it may feel a little uncomfortable at first, but do make the effort to give it your all and do not stop until the seventh question is answered. Before you do your own, I will demonstrate with my example. Please be gentle with yourself as you do this because it is a deeply personal and rather powerful topic to ponder.

Starting statement: *I want to experience the world as much as I possibly can.*

1. Why is this important? *Because I want to live a rich and adventurous life.*
2. Why is this important? *Because I want my time on this Earth to be worth something.*
3. Why is this important? *Because I understand the impermanence of life and want to celebrate the time I was blessed with.*
4. Why is this important? *Because I want my life to have meaning.*
5. Why is this important? *Because I do not want to disappoint myself and feel ungrateful.*
6. Why is this important? *Because I believe each of us is given life to enjoy and not to spoil.*
7. Why is this important? *Because each of us is responsible for our life.*

As you can see, my initial answer differs greatly from the final solution. Of course, this is just one example, and I am certain that under different circumstances, at various stages of life, your 'why' will vary, and that's okay. What is important is to find that 'why' and hold onto it when the storms of life are rocking your boat. Okay, your turn. Write down the first answer and follow the pattern. Try to answer as intuitively as possible. Be courageous and allow yourself to be surprised by your answers. Open your mind and do not criticize or judge what comes up. Just be yourself. For the best results, invite your loved one or a friend to do it with you, so you can have less time to reason your answers and act more intuitively. Are you ready? Let's go!

[WRITE HERE]

Starting Statement:
1. Why is this important?
2. Why is this important?
3. Why is this important?
4. Why is this important?
5. Why is this important?
6. Why is this important?
7. Why is this important?

Alright, with the considered reasons and hopefully a deeper feeling of resolution within our hearts, we are ready to close this chapter and summarize the idea of the 'no matter what' attitude. As self-explanatory as it may be, it will not be easy to pursue unless you have a strong enough reason to do so. Strengthen your character and multiply your chances of success by simply deciding that you will continue trying and striving towards your goals 'no matter what'. Remind yourself of your reasons for this achievement, reflect on your aspirations and their essence often, and do not forget why you started on your journey when the going gets tough and seems too much of a burden to carry on. By commitment and persistence, you are destined to succeed. It may not happen in a week, a month, or a year. It may not happen exactly how you expect it to. It may not happen where and with the means you've prophesized. But it will happen. I am certain of that. Like a drop of water that breaks through rock or an ant that tries to cross an obstacle until it dies, your persistence will certainly propel you in the direction of your goals and make them a reality. Remember that 'a journey of a thousand miles begins with a single step.'[10] If that is the case, then shouldn't we assume that it can also be finished by compounding the total number of these single steps, done consecutively, faithfully, and with great resolve? This, my friend, is the way of the champions.

To continue 'no matter what' is what determines who reaches their destination and who stays behind...

---

[10] Chapter 64 of *Dao De Jing* by Laozi

'You step onto the road, and if you don't keep your feet, there's no knowing where you might be swept off to.'
~ J.R.R. Tolkien in *Lord of the Rings*

Story 18.

"So, what do you think?" the man asked his friend, as they were about to enter the yearly gathering with their colleagues. "When would you consider yourself a successful author...?" The other exhaled the cigarette's smoke and turned his gaze up at the limelight neon above the restaurant's door. "I think once I get on the bestseller list and stay there for at least two years." "Fair enough," his partner responded. "Would that mean this writing adventure of yours is at its finish by then?" The guy stubbed out the cigarette, looked at his friend incredulously, and grinned. "Come on, man, you know the answer to this one... it's only the beginning..."

Later that night, one of the participants announced she was going abroad for some time. "To work and study," she said then. "Let's see which one comes first though..." Laughter followed. This was news to them all, and the conversation meandered back to this new opportunity of the girl from time to time. At some point, as a few of them were about to depart, someone suggested they all go together and stroll down the street for a while. "Those who are not in a hurry, of course," he added. They got up, gathered their things, and paid the bill.

Walking back, the writer approached the girl and smiled. "I'm so happy for you; it's going to be amazing." "Yes, thank you, I hope so," she answered, making up a non-committed smile. "How do you feel about it?" he asked. "I'm a little concerned about it all, you know. Like, what am I going to do if there's no job for me, or if they do not accept me at the university there..." He nodded without saying a word. "They say the first step is the hardest one," she continued, "but I think it's only true until you do that first step, because there are so many more to do, it's crazy..." The man chuckled. "Yeah." "Do you think the first step is the hardest one?" she turned to him. "Eh," he hesitated, "to be honest, I think all of the steps can be quite challenging..." He thought for a moment before picking out the answer. "For example, writing a book may demand of you to write one hundred pages, let's say. You won't be able to write all of them in one go, so you must put it into smaller chunks, two pages a day maybe, maybe three..." She listened intently, and so he continued. "You could say that writing the first one seems the most challenging because you have no idea what you're writing about just yet. But the thing is, that's the case for all of them," he smiled sourly, remembering all the troublesome hours spent in front of that wretched page he both loved and hated, depending on the day. "Quite frankly, I think it's even harder to write the ninetieth page than the first one because the ninetieth one has to fit next to the other eighty-nine..."

They walked on for a few moments without a word. The others were chatting around them. Someone opened a can of beer they hid under their coat. A car horn blared down the street. "So, I guess what I am trying to say is that however hard the first step may feel, you will have to make many more of these steps anyway," he added, taking out the pack of ciggies. "Maybe, then, instead of feeling overwhelmed with any of the steps, from the first till the last one, you should just see them all the same, as little steps, tiny spaces to cross, as you go down the path you've chosen..." "Like writing a book," she smiled. "I like that!" "Like writing a book, one page at a time..."

167

Chapter 18. The First Step Paradox

Have you heard about the idea that the most difficult part of any journey, achievement, or anything you'd like to do is to start...? 'The first step is the hardest thing,' some say; 'to start is the greatest challenge,' others echo. Well, as much as I empathize with the difficulties that the beginnings of anything challenge us with, there is way too much emphasis placed on that 'first step issue' and too little on the fact that there will have to be thousands more such steps taken once you've decided to take that 'walk.' Yet again, please take this chapter lightly and in good faith, as what I am about to say may not be the easiest to hear, but it certainly is something worth noting down and remembering, as you begin on your next great adventure. I am a great believer in the power of habits, in the compounding quality of acting with persistence. As we have mentioned earlier, it is the one simple yet profound quality that often determines success and sifts the 'I wish I would haves' from the 'I am going to's.' Our daily choices determine the outcomes of these ordinary battles. It's just how it is. The great part about it is, as we have noted above, that since it is our daily choice that has the most decision-making power, we are genuinely in charge of it, as long as we are courageous enough to act.

When it comes to starting points, it is often true that for a decision to be made and the wheels to start turning, the first step may seem utterly and overwhelmingly difficult. This is mostly because going into the unknown, leaving the comfort blanket of what we are used to, or changing things that have become our habitual programming is tough. It is, I get it. It is not easy to make a change, especially when it is a major change to make. If you're obese and want to start working out, the first few times at the gym will likely be unpleasant. It may not be too great to hear this, but it is true. The power, however, lies in your decision to do these uncomfortable actions and 'get the ball rolling.' Time will work to your advantage, and if you stick to it, you will get there. I promise.

Now, what do I mean by calling this chapter 'the first step paradox'...? What is so paradoxical about the difficulties and burdens of starting a journey...? Didn't we exhaust this topic already? Well, not exactly. Truth be told, you can look at this 'first step' phenomenon in two ways, and whichever way you decide upon, you will get certain advantages and pay a particular price for it.

Firstly, you can assume that the beginning of anything is, in fact, the hardest part, which when you've done and succeeded in this initial stage, can fuel your enthusiasm and self-confidence with knowing that since you've done the 'most difficult,' everything else will only be easier. It can be very helpful to think in such a way, but it can also be quite a burden in the long run. The price for this kind of attitude comes later—it is deferred. Our motivation peaks at the very beginning of any achievement we put our minds and bodies to. This means that as you start and overcome that first step, you are doing so with the highest potential power in your mind. You are wired to do a great job because the adrenaline, endorphin, and dopamine are rushing through your blood without a stop. You're high on your vision of success, literally. The trouble is, however, that as your journey continues and your enthusiasm comes down a little over time, you may find yourself surprised with the weight that consistent action and overcoming every next challenge carries. And since you've decided that the beginning was the most difficult part, your struggle will seem somehow unfair and unexpected, leaving you greatly distressed and rather demotivated. "What is this!? How can this be so hard?! Shouldn't it be easier already?!", your mind may scream.

There are ways of overcoming this line of thought, but there is an alternative approach to it all, and that's where the paradox may come into play. Let us turn the table and assume that the beginning, as naïve as it may sound, is difficult but far from being the most challenging. There are aspects of starting that make it an arduous, often difficult part, but with the assumption that our goal is greater than just stepping into the gym and doing ten squats, we can consider that initial stage something which has its unique qualities, and that's all there is to it. Instead, let us consider an attitude of courageous anticipation, of being ready for what is yet to come, with the knowledge that what was served as the beginning block for our strength and ability was necessary to become ready for what is yet to come.

The upside of this attitude is quite transparent—you will keep your adrenaline and dopamine levels steadier, knowing that what is yet to come will inevitably become the next great step, and you will try to navigate yourself through these challenges with more humility, knowing that the end is not here yet. The downside, of course, is the other side of the same coin, so to speak. By recognizing that the journey itself will have many ups and downs and all-arounds for us, some of which may completely derail our efforts for a period of time, we are less able to quickly gain the confidence and strengthen our conviction that the path we are treading is the right one to follow. This is a tricky and rather sticky subject because, especially at the beginning of your journey, we will have to walk mostly with the end in mind, rather than visible results of any kind.

Working out for a week won't make you see the results of your effort. You will have to continue with it for a month, two, maybe more, to even start witnessing the payoffs of your struggle. The beginning, and your resilience throughout it, depends on your confidence in the goal and the courageous faith to 'keep at it.' It can quickly become an arduous effort if you forget that it takes much more than a week or two to see anything worthwhile changing for the better. Nothing worthwhile happens overnight.

There is, however, an important thing to note here, which causes me to believe that applying the second attitude can be a more sustainable and long-term-ready approach to these dreams of ours. As we have mentioned earlier, you can either choose the first step as a springboard in gaining confidence in your reasons and powering through the challenges, or as a checkpoint, which marks the beginning of a marathon, which offers such a checkpoint of satisfaction and confidence every now and then, but for the most part of the journey is impossible to anticipate. Both approaches are good enough, and both will get you to your goal, as long as you keep at it, of course. Personally, I prefer the second attitude more because it places less emphasis on what has been done and what is happening here and now and invites you to look forward, down the road, to gaze at the horizon, instead of watching your feet or looking back. Try running a marathon with either of these gaze focal points and see which works best. I guess you could argue that the best way to run is to look a few meters in front of you, so you can avoid the rocks, slippery parts, and little ditches, which is a fair point. I appreciate that. Let us find the middle ground in it all. You neither look too far over the horizon nor too close to your feet. Just a few meters ahead. That works for me.

What I want you to remember and practice, however, especially in the mental part of this journey of yours, is that where you are heading is more important than where you have been and where you are now. We need to recognize where we are, so we can tell where we should go next, but our past is only useful to the extent it allows us to understand ourselves. Nothing more. In this case, your first step is nothing more than the humble resolution, a gesture of faith, that where you aim to go is possible for you, and you are on your way. You know there will be many more such steps to come, many of which will smack you in the face and put you out of balance, but these are all temporary. Everything is. So, do not hang on too much to the idea of starting and the difficulty of it. It will be challenging, that's true, but it won't get any easier if you constantly ponder the overwhelming radicality of your striving.

Think of it like learning to swim in the pool. Starting is overcoming the crippling fear that stops you from getting into the water. You may use the ladder, jump in, or slide from the side. You have dealt with the initial fear, but at least four more appear. You are still holding onto the side, refuse to let go of your parent's or coach's hand, and maybe you are also without goggles on your face because that's a great reason for everyone to see that you are not ready just yet. 'Just a few moments more,' you cry. Taking this first step was difficult, but you are far from the success you're looking for. To become a swimmer, you will have to let go of the side, risk getting your eyes slightly achy, understand the tempo of your breath, learn to synchronize your movements, and probably deal with the greatest fear each of us must face – the fear of death. Doesn't sound too pretty, does it? But that, my friend, is how you learn to swim. And that is how you learn to do anything and everything. That is how you succeed.

So, take that first step now, but don't give it too much of your attention. Do not give it any more power over you than it needs to take. Use it as an adrenaline, dopamine, and endorphin boost but do not hang onto it for too long. Take the second step the moment the first one is done. Keep playing the cards you're dealt. Get away from the side. Let go of your comfort zone. Experiment, fall on your face with grace, smile towards the horizon, do not look down on your feet too much, and above all, never, never look back while you run. It will not only slow you down, but it will also most likely make you fall. And we both know falling on concrete isn't pretty. So, remember to not let yourself fall prey of that 'first step paradox'…

'Learn to do everything lightly. Yes, feel lightly even though you're feeling deeply.
Just lightly let things happen and lightly cope with them.'
~ Aldous Huxley

Story 19.

They were about to board the plane, coming back from an intense, adventure-filled week in the seaside city of Portugal. There were three of them: three friends coming back home after a week worth of experiences, en route to their city of residence. Each of them was struggling with his own little challenge that afternoon. One had not slept longer than ten minutes in the past thirty-six hours, which made standing in the queue, checking passports, running for the bus, and packing luggage quite an effort on his part. The second one was totally ill. After a week without much rest and a lack of healthy food, his body gave up, succumbing to the common cold, which quickly escalated to a flu-like state. He, even more so, struggled to stand still and keep a straight face throughout their journey. The third one was still drunk. Out of the three states, this could be considered the least straining one, as, for the most part, he did not suffer much due to his silly, slightly sleep-deprived humour, to which he switched upon awakening a few hours earlier. With the amount of alcohol, he had consumed the night before, there was no doubt he was going to continue the sobering process as they journeyed on.

Standing there, in the long queue of mask-faced passengers on the way to the plane, the three tried to keep one another vertical with sheer will and a few last bursts of energy. The sick one was truly in trouble, trying to stop himself from coughing, cleaning his nose every ten seconds, and trying to weather this stormy moment by covering his ears with the sweet sounds of the songs he so dearly appreciated. The other two helped him to stand tall. They formed a rather miserable picture for those who were there to watch. "I'm so tired my mind clicks in and out from moment to moment," one of them stated, *"it's like I'm micro-sleeping at times..." "Standing, sitting, I don't know,"*[11] *murmured the drunken one with a slight chuckle at the end, as he recalled a silly quote from a series they all loved, "we're going home boys, we are going home..." The third one was silent.*

"It was worth it though, wasn't it?" the boy looked at his mellow friend, "it was a crazy, worthwhile adventure." "Definitely," the other nodded, "no doubt about it!" They smiled slightly, and the third one must have noticed their exchange, as he pulled off one of the headphone's ears and made an effort to speak through the muffle of the mask, "this might just be the most miserable state I have ever been in..." The two looked at one another for a moment, before they quietly laughed with their strained throats. Their chuckle must have sounded more like a desperate whine since some queuing passengers looked over at them. They smiled at those strangers in return. "You're doing great, brother," one of them turned to the ill one, "just keep standing strong, we are almost there; this will be a hell of a story to tell one day!" Another raspy burst of laughter followed. They boarded the plane after some time, sat in their seats, and fell silent. The sleep-deprived one fell asleep almost instantly, the drunken one tried to calm his approaching hangover with a bottle of water, and the ill one was trying to let go of the sensations the disease was causing. He must have struggled quite a bit during that trip. He must have.

---

[11] Quote from Season 1, Episode 8 of *Rick and Morty*

Upon arriving home, they went their separate ways without much of a word. They were all destroyed, either through disease, lack of rest, or overindulgence. They were completely trashed. The two went to their flat and the third one lived alone. They climbed up the staircase and opened the door with a loud exhale of relief on the ill one's side. They were home.

"Home sweet home," the 'still healthy' one announced. "Goddamn... what a trip, eh?" "You go to bed straight away. I'll make us tea and give you some medicine also," he commanded his suffering colleague. "We are already home, brother. Now's the time to rest, recuperate, and renew." He laughed. "You'll feel like a new man tomorrow," he added. "Rest to fight another day..."

Chapter 19. Take It Lightly

Since the beginning of our little journey, we have been quite serious about the things we discussed. We considered all the reasons we may have for success, explored the ways in which each of us can calm and recognize their inner world with simple activities, talked about strategies for overcoming obstacles, dismissing failures, and striving for a better tomorrow, and pondered the inevitability of the hustle that awaits all those who decide to walk their own path. In other words, we have been quite intense. I hope you are feeling okay, regardless, and that our discussion so far has not disheartened your spirit of enthusiasm and progress. And even if it did, as much as I may be sorry for that, I trust that by sticking with it for a little longer, you will see that it is all just a great game in which you hopefully want to join me.

In the world of so many distractions, disturbances, and suffering, it is rather challenging to 'take things lightly'. It is especially difficult to do so when we witness people around us, the planet, or any other part of our Universe in trouble. Our good nature expects us to help, to pick up the pace, to give up our time in the name of the greater good, to commit to a lifestyle of efficiency and voluntary help for all involved. We are driven to make the world a better place, and that is truly both fascinating and wonderful. The trouble, however, arises when this drive to support and help everyone everywhere every time disables us from taking sufficient care of our own wellbeing.

What I am going to propose may not be what you'd like to hear, but bear with me. Since you've gone so far with me on this journey,

I trust that our relationship of openness and understanding can help us both weather the essence of this chapter. Let me invite you to become a selfless selfish person because if you do not, you will find yourself fighting with the windmills of chaos without a chance of success.

Have you ever thought why the first rule of First Aid refers to 'checking the surroundings' and 'making sure you are safe'? The answer to this question can also be found in the plane emergency plan instructions, which invite you to 'first put on your oxygen mask before you assist your children or others around you'. It is all about pragmatism and the likelihood of your help truly being helpful and not quite the opposite. Just think about it – what use would anyone have of your first aid if by approaching the injured victim, you get yourself injured and rendered incapable of helping? Wouldn't that be slightly off the mark with your goal of helping them recover? It's not like you can carry anyone out of the danger zone if you get hit by the car and join their troublesome state.

This is where I would like to start our selfless selfish discourse. This is where I want you to begin considering just how much of your help to others can be truly helpful depending on your circumstances and attitude. Good examples of this approach can be found in such trivial activities as saving a little change or consuming coffee. Let's consider how good it is to advise others on their spending habits when our own account is suffering from a negative bottom line. Similarly, who are we to tell others how much coffee they should drink or how many spoons full of sugar is 'enough' for their health if our habit is preventing us from sleeping well and influences our mood swings as we crave that cup first thing in the morning? I am not saying you should tell others how to do their things even after you've become the healthiest, wealthiest version of yourself you could have become, but your help to them will be much more likely to help if it comes from the place of your own experience and success, rather than from the space of intelligent consideration without any proof of its work.

So, let us take everything we do and invite others to do with a pinch of salt, and reflect on this idea of first 'taking care of yourself' before we interrupt the journey of others or try to fix the world with our actions. As one great man famously stated, "If you want to change the world, start your day by making your bed."[12] Or, alternatively, "Get your house in order before you criticize the world."[13] Now, do not consider this as discouragement from doing your best to make the world around you better, but as advice on where to start if you wish to do so. And that's where we come to the major trick of this chapter—taking things lightly.

As you may have noticed already, there will be times in your life when your daily effort, your will to help, your tiresome struggle, and any other exerted power of yours seem to go no further than beyond your reach. You may want to help your friend become a healthier person, and you do your all trying to get them to work out with you, participate in extra activities, eat better, and more regularly. You invest your attention, intention, and time in them, and you get no results. This may feel discouraging, demeaning even, and slowly but surely, you may start blaming yourself for not

---

[12] *Make Your Bed* by Admiral William H. McRaven

[13] *12 Rules for Life: An Antidote to Chaos* by Jordan B. Peterson

being able to help or them for not being willing to participate. Either way, you are now negatively influencing your relationship (with yourself or others) because of this initiative that simply could not work, even if you were to give your 200% in place of the 100 you already gave.

You may wonder, why do I think that? Well, let me tell you something that I've had to learn the hard way, again and again, and still, after all these years of passionate search for the most efficient ways of inspiring myself and others to improve our lives, I fall into this trap from time to time. PEOPLE DO NOT CHANGE UNLESS THEY ARE WILLING TO DO SO. You cannot teach someone anything unless they are open to learning it. You cannot help someone with their problem unless they want to find a solution. You cannot make someone adopt a habit unless they are willing to change. And the most ironic part of it is, it applies to yourself as well! Yes, you heard me! You may read all the books about healthy life you want, you may go to all the 'most efficient abs-building classes' you find, you may try all the 'one and only supplements for cutting weight' there are, but if you do not change your attitude and truly agree with yourself that such change should and is going to occur, it won't. And even if it does, it will be momentary because instead of digging out the roots and replanting your approach, you've just shaved half of the plant and left it in the same place to regain its shape in no time.

I know this may sound brutal, but it really isn't. Relax. Chill out! Your stress and 'no pain, no gain' attitude won't cut it. It will only make you more stressed and drive you to premature burnout. At this stage of the book, we both know you're no quitter—you've explored many aspects of lively attitudes with me, and I trust you've done the tasks as invited. Since we are so far down the road (and ahead of others, as it is estimated that only about 10% of people worldwide actually write down and decide on their long-term goals and commitments), it is time to slow down and ponder this journey you've embarked on. Your approach to success is the most powerful force you have up your sleeve. It's the card you should always play and become its closest friend. And the best part is, it can apply to anything in life, not only to success.

Choose an activity, an aspect of your existence, or an invention you've been thinking about, apply your attitude of enthusiasm and trust into it, and see how it grows, transforms, and becomes. 'Attention energizes, intention transforms'[14]—do not ever forget that. But, as we have been discussing in this chapter, you need to also give way for the nature of things to do its job without pushing and pulling on the different strands of your dreamwork in the meantime. That's where the idea of 'taking things lightly' can really help. Both in terms of working with others and with yourself, you may find moments when things seem not to go your way, someone may be opposing your idea, or the intention you've placed shatters instead of becoming a beautiful mirror. Everything is a work in progress, always. Even the greatest works of art, business, and philosophy are nothing more than works in progress because they could be improved indefinitely if you were to continue working on them. But that's the point, why would you? Wouldn't it feel better to leave the project done almost perfectly (as perfection doesn't really exist) and continue your journey with the next exciting

---

[14] *The Seven Spiritual of Success* by Deepak Chopra

work? By allowing your attitude of enthusiasm to stay strong, while offering space for the 'taking things lightly' approach to also participate, you will not feel discouraged by another, you will avoid conflict about things that are yours to decide and no one else has an actual say about them, and you will feel less stress, as your efforts to better your life will be subjected only to your own judgment, even if condemnation from those around you comes. After all, they have their own opinions, attitudes, and priorities, and that's none of your business. But neither is your joy a business of theirs.

Remember what we said earlier—you won't change anyone's opinion unless they decide to change it themselves—so there is no point in you struggling and tugging on that rope to pull them to your side when all they want to do is sit there in their comfort zone of ignorance. I want to warn you because this kind of situation will happen often as you go through the chapters of your life. People who do not feel comfortable stepping out of their safe space will likely try to quiet you or pull you into their cozy blanket of passivity, because seeing you strive, and change can cause them some pain of self-disappointment. And no, they won't notice it is their fault and problem; they will project it onto you, as you were the one triggering their painful thoughts… That is why, stay away from them, if need be, and beware.

I often notice that whenever I share my ideas and works with others, I get one of these two responses in return, each of them tricky in their own way. On one hand, those who cheer you on and are excited for you can add a great boost to your efforts, but, as we have explored in Chapter 12, by sharing your plans too much, you may actually slow down your progress, as their excitement and encouragement can provide your brain with enough dopamine that you feel satisfied and celebrate the success, which has not happened yet. On the other hand, by sharing your plans or vision of the future with those who (1) do not feel comfortable with themselves, (2) do not wish you well, (3) do not know what to do themselves, you may actually put your goals in danger of negative influence, both in a metaphysical and physical sense of the word. We've discussed this briefly before, but let me remind you: people who do not feel satisfied with themselves are likely to dislike your efforts of making your situation better – this is because your action suggests that they also could do it, and puts them in a position of weakness, which only they can really see, feel, and suffer from. Secondly, if (for any reason) your conversation partner does not actually wish you well, your exposure of plans and dreams can be the first step of their sabotage. You've literally handed the weapon to your enemy without knowing it, which is one of the greatest mistakes one can make both in war, business, and social relations. Finally, the person who hears your plans and ideas may not have any idea of their own. This impotence of their potential can truly cause them to suffer, which will (yet again) likely spill out in the form of resentment towards you, as the person who triggered the pain. It's pretty much the same story as the first example. Either way, you're the problem, and they may want to take care of you, so they do not have to take care of their real problem. In any of these situations, if you've already 'spilled the milk,' it is best to take things lightly and remember the philosophy of the ant. You are going to get there no matter what, so someone badmouthing you or sabotaging your efforts should not be too much of an issue. Your focus should be placed on keeping in touch with your feelings, taking care of your mental strength, and continuing the journey, regardless of who must be left behind.

The irony of this situation is that many people will follow you when they see their actions cannot change your trajectory. The most important part, however, is to take off from the ground and exit their stratosphere, before they pull you back down, because they are too scared to fly themselves. So, take things lightly and understand that everyone has a different story and their own 'cross' to bear. Accept that your actions may offend some people and inspire others. Do not try to convince or force anyone to do anything against their will. Realize that your work is yours to take care of and no one else's. Trust the process, avoid talking about your plans and ideas to people you're unsure of, and believe in your story, even if everyone around you is urging you to stop. They may wish you well, but sometimes well-wishing is a positive twist on a chaos-causing attitude. Do not allow others to influence your wind, stay strong like the willow tree, and bend against the tide, but never break. That's the way towards success, with grace and self-care.
Do your thing, respect others and don't forget to take things lightly…

'All we have to decide is what to do
with the time that is given us.'
~ J.R.R. Tolkien in *Lord of the Rings*

Story 20.

"Do you know if you'll ever live back home again?" his friend asked him one day, as they were about to go home after a night-time gathering. "I'm not sure, man," he answered, "I have yet to decide, but the truth is, I'm not sure if I will be the one to decide..." "Life happens for us, you know," he added. They were talking about the different adventures each of them had been going through over the past few years. The boy had been away for a fifth of his life already, and considering the accelerating rate at which time was perceived by both of them, they had plenty to tell one another. There was a lot to "catch up" on. Some of their friends were already getting married, some had their careers worked out, some bought houses, and even had babies. The two were going at their own pace. One was a professional trainer and a part-owner of a gym, the other a starting journalist, a writer-to-be. Both, from the same neighbourhood. Both with a shared past.

"Anything unusual you have learned from all these journeys so far?" his friend changed the subject, trying to lighten up the solemn mood which followed the consideration of time flying by. "Umm, I'm not sure," he answered, "a few things interested me, but if there is any lesson about it all..." He fell silent, pondering. His friend picked up the backpack and stood up from the bench, waiting for the answer. "I kind of feel nothing really matters, you know," he finally spoke, "not in a negative sense, but more like in general..." "We give things meaning, and so they matter to us, but in the end, they don't really matter at all," he continued, "I don't think we do either..."

The other one stood there for a moment, hanging onto the words that echoed throughout their minds. "Hmm," he hesitated, "that sounds deep and rather deflating, man..." "It doesn't have to, though," the boy countered, "it doesn't have to..." Silently considering the idea, the two weighed their beliefs, considerations, and experiences regarding the doubtful meaning of anything in the Universe, which they found themselves in. "Would you say it feels any better to think that?" his friend asked, unconvinced. The boy thought for a moment. "No, but that's not the point either..." "It's not about feeling any better; there are two layers or more to it all," he added, "on one hand, I recognize that nothing has inherent meaning, which is somewhat obvious if you dismiss the subjective point of view, but at the same time, because we can and we do, anything can have deeper meaning because we choose to give it just that; we decide what has meaning to us..."

"I see," the other pounced on the opportunity to lighten the mood, "that's some thoughtful thing you said there, you know...?" "Might be worth putting it in a book or something," he added. The boy nodded with a slight smile and got up as well. They shook hands and started towards their cars. "I hope it will get there one day," he said as he was walking away, "it would mean the world to me..." "I bet it will," his friend said, opening his car's door, "and I look forward to reading it..."

Chapter 20. Without Meaning

I wonder how you are feeling after all these adventures of ours so far. Have you discovered anything new about yourself as you continued this literary journey with me? Do you feel any better than before this book fell into your hands? Have you had a chance to notice the changes happening around you as the changes within you have taken place? Did you at least have fun, or was it not that much of a big deal for you after all? Was I simply repeating things you've already known from before? Did I annoy you with my writing? I hope I didn't, but of course, you are free to feel however you fancy, and if so, I am sorry for stirring these kinds of emotions within you. Whatever your experience with me might have been, I am very grateful you've joined me on this journey. For me, it was a great adventure and a worthy one. I've learned so much and was able to put into words, organize into sentences, and apply in life, all these things we've been discussing. I've learned a lot thanks to you, so thank you for helping me go through with it. Really, I mean it.

The last chapter of our consideration trip will hopefully be the first one of your own next adventure. I think it is safe to say that all things have their beginning and their end, and it can be both rather morbid and greatly relieving to realize it. Before we part our ways, I want you to explore with me one last aspect of this whole story of life we've been talking about. I want us to feel okay with ourselves to the healthy extent one should, and I have not found a better way of putting things into perspective but by seeing the impermanence and utter meaninglessness in the essence of our existence. I know it may sound upsetting, but bear with me, please (I know, you know, you can trust me at this point).

Each of us came to this mysterious world quite surprisingly lucky. The mere fact you made it this far means you won plenty of Universal lotteries in the chemistry of life because the likelihood of being born is an astonishingly tiny number in comparison to what we tend to call luck or fortitude. Moreover, since you managed to get here and you're reading this, you are probably one of the privileged who can read, write, and have access to the channels that allowed this little book of mine to fall into your hands. It is no small thing, you know…? I am truly humbled by realizing just how many advantages I was handed whenever I notice the poverty, misfortune, or pure bad luck in the world around me. I hope that by the time you'll be reading these words, fewer beings will be suffering on Earth, but who knows…

This radical luck, which you and I have found ourselves in, has one more, majestically wondrous, chronically overwhelming, and statistically absurd quality. Our lives, in the most essential essence of them, at their very deepest core, are rather meaningless. We are born, we live, and then we die. We may live again in another life, who knows…?! I quite like that idea, but let us stick to the facts for now. We come here for a fraction of a millisecond, if you consider just how old the Earth is and how many generations of people came and left before us. It truly takes the tiniest moment of the Universe's time to keep me and you around. We don't really matter much on the grand scale, you know…? If I were to stop at this point, you would probably throw this book across the room, if you haven't yet, and mumble a few offensive words towards someone who had the audacity of saying that your life is meaningless at its core. Well, I hope you haven't just yet, and that you are ready to hear the bright side of this coin. As we have mentioned and you are certainly aware of already, everything can be seen from a different perspective, and a big part of finding joy and satisfaction in life comes from being able to see it from the perspective we wish to observe it from.

That is why I present to you the philosophy of meaning, which has kept me going through many hardships and will be there for me through many more yet to come. Inevitably. Consider the freedom you are blessed with. Think about just how much potential for choice you've been granted since, in the essence of it all, you do not matter that much. Your life is yours. That's the ultimate truth. Nothing too secret or surprising about it. It's basic knowledge, right?! Well, I wonder, why are we not reminding ourselves of this when something goes sideways for us? Why do we mull over petty stuff, get annoyed at one another so easily, or get obsessed about a job that does not matter in the slightest? Why do we care so much for so little?

Instead, I want to invite you to take my literary hand and walk with me down the aisle reserved for those who decide their own fate. Since there is nothing essentially meaningful about your life, you are in charge of choosing, creating, and sustaining meaning for yourself. The meaning of life is life itself, and in that, my friend, you are the captain of your lively boat. You choose your direction; you choose what your life could mean. Over the time you're blessed to spend on this spinning rock in the vacuum of the Universe, you are going to be asked, expected, pushed, invited, and considered for many roles, jobs, activities, groups, situations, opportunities, challenges, and anything in between. Sometimes you will slip and fall, sometimes you will climb up and look down with triumph. Most times, you will simply take on another mundane day of whatever your life is currently about and make it your own. And this is where my invitation to remember that nothing really matters comes in handy.

Let me make this clear: you are not required to be, have, do, or want anything that you do not choose to. It is all up to you. Of course, there will be times when circumstance will make you work on something a little less exciting than your greatest dream, but as long as you keep that destination in your mind, and you recognize, again and again, that your life has meaning only because you are alive and is not determined by any external factors, you will be free from the greatest concern the world is struggling with. You will be free from the concern caused by "other's expectations of you."

There is also a great advantage hidden beneath this essentially meaningless life philosophy, which allows us to get over our troubles with less suffering. By reminding yourself that you are ultimately here only for a moment and that all which is, was not at some point in time, and will not be any more soon enough, you will feel less attachment and grief when a thing does not go as planned, or you lose something or someone you value. This does not mean you will not feel pain when a loved one dies. That's a given, if you loved them, because what you are experiencing is the love itself – the grief that comes with a loved one's departure is your love, which goes through the turmoil, as the immediate access to that person's physicality is lost. They may be gone from this plane of existence, but I have not found any reasons not to keep my hopes up about there being another plane waiting for all of us. Feel free to take this with you as well, if it helps, or explore this concept further on your own. Whatever you believe, you give meaning to, and that is why your faith in yourself is the purest and probably most appropriate belief you can ever grant your privileged luck of being born. You were given a chance to be here, and you were offered the ability to choose your attitude toward every single moment of your life. Doesn't that make you powerful beyond imagination?

I would like to finish with this idea: wherever you go, whatever you may do, it is ultimately up to you how you're going to experience it. Any pain can be transformed into meaningful suffering, any shortcoming can become a shortcut towards achievement, and any obstacle can be an opportunity for you to become a better person. Everything can be anything in the eyes of the beholder. If that isn't true, then I do not know what is. You are in charge of but one thing in this world – yourself. By choosing your attitude, deciding on your priorities, believing in yourself, and acting in the direction you've chosen, you will be successful in living a meaningful life – YOUR MEANINGFUL LIFE. And there is no one else you need to convince about its meaning. Moreover, apart from your loved ones, for whom you are essentially meaningful because they love you, nobody cares about anyone else more than they do about themselves, so do not waste your time and effort trying to convince the whole world that you are special. I know you are. You know you are. Those who care about you know you are. Whether anyone else knows that is irrelevant. Live your life and give it the meaning it deserves. It's as simple as that…

Remember that since all is without inherent meaning, it is up to you what becomes meaningful FOR YOU.

THE END

Epilogue

While writing these words, I've been slowly coming to terms with the emotions and thoughts my world has been filled with recently. What started as a little story for children spun into a full-blown book for people who are ready to think for themselves and leave the world in the rear-view mirror of their perspective vehicle. I would sit down each morning, ponder the turmoil of intention and attention I was going through that day, and upon writing, I would find the words that would soothe my mind a little. Sometimes by making me happy, sometimes by forcing me to realize the needed change, which had to take place as soon as possible. They were moments of self-reflection and self-care, which, in the long run, allowed me to withstand the many challenges my present life would throw at me. Most importantly, they kept me sane.

In a world full of people and connections, we are progressively alienating ourselves from others. This is true especially for the younger generations and those who are yet to come. I, myself, am lucky and blessed enough to have a great number of deeply loving friends and family, who have been my safety net for as long as I can remember. Without my parents, my siblings, my family, and my friends, I would be, as many people are nowadays, lost and depressed. Without their presence, support, and appreciation, I would be no more.

It suffices to say, that by becoming more aware of ourselves, we become more vulnerable. Ignorance is bliss, after all. If you do not know about something that would make you wonder whether the choices, you're making are the right ones, you do not suffer the inner turmoil about these choices. The more we know, the more prone to suffering we are. That is why so many people all over the world would rather sit in front of a TV and not think at all than ponder the meaning of their life. Because ultimately, our lives are only as meaningful as we make them, and that puts plenty of responsibility on us. And who wants more responsibility these days, anyway…?

My journey of self-awareness and self-care has only just begun. I am but a young man, who, through my love for the world and affection for the power of words, was drawn to the page, which somehow, at some point, became a welcoming and reassuring comfort blanket to the angst of existence. With each word offered out into the ether of the world, I feel a little more hope that by helping ourselves, we can help others, who in turn will be able to help people they encounter. I wish to see people smiling wider, look up from their phones more often, talk to one another in the elevators, and give way on the intersections instead of blaring their horns as if the end of the world was upon us. Maybe it is, I sometimes think. Maybe it isn't. If you think about it, it doesn't really matter. Worrying about the future is only certain to make us miserable in the present. That's all.

Instead of this, I hope we, the community of this planetary species, will be able to come together in a more appreciative and understanding dialogue. I hope us to be okay with one another and stop the many absurd conflicts over nothing but greed, ignorance, and fear. It is rather difficult to get into a fight with another when what you are feeling annoyed about is recognized as an unimportant detail in the meaningless life of yours. Instead, put your attention and intention into the loving and creative behaviours, thoughts, and emotions you want to feel. Because that's what it's all about, right...? Feeling. Experiencing. Living. All of us want to feel healthy, happy, safe, and loved. Everything else can be found in the cherry on top of the wonderful carrot cake (yes, I love carrot cake, hence the choice) we call life.

And that's what I would like to wish for you, my dear reader, listener, or a curious bystander who is right now peeking over the shoulder of the reader of this book - to be healthy, happy, safe, and loved. I hope you may find peace with yourself, choose your life's meaning, and make your dreams come true. And I wish I have done my part in helping you achieve either of these. Thank you for joining me on my journey.
Till next time.

I wish you all the best and will see you in this life or the next.

Sincerely,
Wojciech Salski

About The Autor

For as long as I can remember, I have been telling stories. Some were more interesting than others, some fit the situation, and some did not. Learning about myself, I soon decided to pursue a career within the realm of my passion for storytelling.

I write, film, and record, making the necessary mistakes and 'quantum leaps' along the way. Philosophy and art have been the biggest inspiration for most, if not all, of my works.

I believe that each of us has many great stories to tell, and I think it is our mission to do so.

That is why through storytelling, I am trying to make the world a better place, one word at a time…

 If you have enjoyed this book and would like to explore more of my works, scan the QR code.

There, you can find:

(Un)usual Stories – my first **book**, published in 2021.

(Un)usual Stories – a weekly **podcast** started in 2020.

You can also reach out to me by sending an email to: **contact@salski.pl**

www.ingramcontent.com/pod-product-compliance
Lightning Source LLC
Chambersburg PA
CBHW032128160426
43197CB00008B/559